PRAISE FOR
The Game of Their Lives

"Worthy of comparison to such classics of sports reporting as David Halberstam's *Summer of '49*, this book should be a real kick for soccer rooters and nonfans alike."   —*Kirkus Reviews*

"[Douglas] excels and becomes almost poetic . . . in his depiction of life in the ethnic big-city ghettos."   —*Publishers Weekly*

"Douglas does a superb job in not only retelling the contest but chronicling the lives of these humble few in the years following the match. A refreshing tale of sporting heroes: no pretensions, no glamour, no high salaries, just ordinary people playing a game they love. This is a good, heartwarming read."   —*Library Journal*

Mary Lou Hubbell

About the Author

GEOFFREY DOUGLAS is a former newspaper publisher, editor, columnist, and reporter whose work has also appeared in many magazines. He is the author of two critically acclaimed books, *Class: The Wreckage of an American Family* and *Dead Opposite: The Lives and Loss of Two American Boys*. Douglas teaches writing at the University of Massachusetts and lives in southern New Hampshire.

The

GAME OF
THEIR LIVES

The

GAME OF
THEIR LIVES

The Untold Story of the
World Cup's Biggest Upset

G E O F F R E Y   D O U G L A S

itbooks

AN IMPRINT OF HARPERCOLLINS PUBLISHERS

Originally published in 1996 by Henry Holt and Company, Inc.

HarperCollins books may be purchased for educational, business, or sales promotional use. For information please write: Special Markets Department, HarperCollins Publishers Inc., 10 East 53rd Street, New York, NY 10022.

First Perennial Currents edition published 2005.

Designed by Michelle McMillan

Library of Congress Cataloging-in-Publication Data is available upon request.

ISBN 0-06-075877-5

09 RRD 10 9 8

To Charley Columbo, Joe Gaetjens, Joe Maca,
Ed McIlenny, Eddie Sousa, and Frank Wallace.
Your silence has been a privilege to fill.

Author's Note

When I set out two years ago to write this book, I expected to be writing a story of remembrances: of a time, a soccer game, a way of life long past. To begin with, that's all I intended—a story rooted in nostalgia, a celebration of forgotten things.

The book is all of that—but something else too. Something I couldn't have foreseen (much less intended) before I had met and spent time with the five men whose words fill most of its pages. It is a story of lives wonderfully well lived. Of a team of young men (there were eleven to begin with) who once played a game brilliantly but obscurely—asking nothing of it but joy, and whatever wins might come along—then went on to live (and die) in exactly the same way. It is a story of lives of the quietest sort of glory, whose largest celebrations have come in damp locker rooms, family kitchens, the waiting rooms of maternity wards.

"Breakup" is the catchword of our times—the breakup of families, of neighborhoods, of communities and traditions, of everything in a society that binds one life to another and makes life itself a hopeful, precious thing. Our newsstands and bookstores burgeon with the accounts of all that happens when these ties no longer bind (I myself have written one such book)—welfare families, teenage mothers, battered women, "wilding," hate crimes, the culture of sneakers and drugs. Grim, graphic indices of a society eroding from within.

But there is a flip side. The reverse of breakup is cohesion. So where are the stories of the lives that have cohered? Is the intact family always the happier one? Do its sons grow up to be better fathers? Better husbands? Happier men? Has a neighborhood the power to nurture? Or a church the power to unite? Can a supper table be a festive place when there are only potatoes to eat?

I had no answers to such questions before I came to know these men. Two years later, *thanks* only to knowing them, I feel certain that I do.

It is for this—more even than for the time they gave me or the memories they shared—that I thank them: Walter Bahr, Frank Borghi, Harry Keough, Gino Pariani, Clarkie Sousa. It has been a privilege to tell their stories.

I am indebted, too, to the wives and families of these men (especially Alma Keough, Rosemary Borghi, and Anita Sousa) for sharing their homes and their time, and the fullness of their remembrances.

And to the Ravens—they know who they are—for the lunch they would not let me buy, and the wonderful, warm glimpses of friendship it offered.

Some published sources have been indispensable: *The Ultimate Encyclopedia of Soccer,* edited by Keir Radnedge (Rocklin, Calif.: Prima Publishing, 1995); *The Grass of Another Country,* by Christopher Merrill (New York: Henry Holt, 1993); and, most especially, *Immigrants on the Hill,* by Gary R. Mormino (Champaign: University of Illinois Press, 1986), to my mind the prototype of what every collection of oral histories should be.

And thanks to the U.S. National Soccer Hall of Fame in Oneonta, New York, and its director, Albert Colone, for the technical support and photos they provided.

Yes, it is fiercely difficult for the athlete to grow old, but to age with dignity and with courage cuts close to what it is to be a man. And most of them have aged that way, with dignity, with courage and with hope.

—from *The Boys of Summer*, Roger Kahn

The
GAME OF
THEIR LIVES

1

The playing field wasn't much to look at or to play on. There would be reports later in the British press that it was a converted bullring, but this couldn't have been so—they have never fought bulls in Brazil. Still, the grass was parched and patchy, and far too high in spots. The ball, instead of settling, teed up unnaturally on the tufts. There were likely to be overkicks.

The stands were of brick and timber, built a generation before the war. It was said that they groaned and swayed slightly when full—though it took only 30,000 to fill them, not the 50,000 or 60,000 that would be reported in the press. Even so, there wasn't an empty seat that day.

The locker rooms were cramped, foul smelling, and cobweb-filled. The English had disdained them; they'd arrived already dressed. The Americans were less fussy. They'd seen worse.

Of all of Brazil's major stadiums, this one was the humblest. Only first-round matches were to be played here, and only the least of those—the mismatches and second-level games. In this case a mismatch: the worst against the best.

The place was Belo Horizonte (Beautiful Horizon), a mining city of two million, three hundred miles north of Rio—though there was no horizon in sight. The city, founded in the gold rush of the 1790s on the backs of Indian slaves, is a day's drive inland and surrounded on every side by hills.

"From the moment we landed there," Tom Finney, who played outside-right for the English team, would tell reporters later, "nothing was real, nothing was quite right. It was as if we had flown into some strange, impossible fantasy land."

The crowd had come to root against the English. Or at least to vilify them—there being no chance, none at all, that they would lose. They were the "Reyes de Futbol" (Kings of Soccer), as the local paper had called them that week. It would take a *miraculo* for the "Pobres Americanos" to stay within six goals.

But that was only part of the point. As the youngest boy in the stands that day knew, if there were any team on Earth that could challenge the English, it would be the Brazilians themselves. That match would come later—in the final round-of-four—though none doubted that it would come. In the meantime, the 30,000 were there that morning as much to measure as to root.

The date was June 29, 1950, a Thursday. The year and the century were half done. Across most of Brazil, inflation had flattened the dreams raised briefly by a wartime boom. Its people, in a national election three months hence, would return their hopes to a deposed dictator, Getúlio Vargas, who would end his term in disgrace, then suicide, less than four years after that.

In the United States, meanwhile, the headlines were of one thing only. North Korea, four days earlier, had crossed the thirty-eighth parallel. Before nightfall the next day—June 30—President Truman would commit forces, and America would be at war.

In New York, the Yankees, behind Berra, Rizzuto, and a fading DiMaggio (the Mantle years were still to come), were en route to another pennant, their tenth in fifteen years; three months later, they would sweep the Series from the Phillies in four straight. Willie Mays, a year shy of his rookie season, was a nineteen-year-old out-fielder in the Negro National League. Joe Louis, thirty-six and rumored to be broke, was in training for a comeback—which would end sadly ten weeks later at the hands of Ezzard Charles.

The Brinks robbery, six months old and still unsolved, was "the crime of the century." *Death of a Salesman* had just closed on Broadway; *All About Eve* would be Best Picture of the Year.

And four months earlier, in Wheeling, West Virginia, an obscure forty-one-year-old senator from Wisconsin had made national headlines with the charge that the U.S. State Department was a hotbed of Reds.

The world's population was two and a half billion. For perhaps a twelfth of them that June morning, the only news that mattered was on the soccer fields of Brazil. It was week one, day six, of the World Cup—the first in twelve years, since play had been halted for war.

Every day for twenty-two days—from the twenty-fifth of June to the sixteenth of July—from pressrooms in the stadiums of Rio, Recife, Brasilia, São Paulo, Curitiba, and Belo Horizonte, four hundred reporters from forty nations would transmit their accounts:

The Swedes, paced by the "wondrous" Nacka Skoglund, had shocked favored Italy and were now the tourney's "sleeping lion." . . .

Spain was playing "timorously." Paraguay was "the Latins' mystery team." . . .

England's Stanley Matthews, "the Wizard of Dribble," was to be "rested" against the United States. He had "limped briefly" against Chile—would he be ready against Spain? . . .

The Brazilians, under coach Flavio Costa, were "sleeping under cotton wool" with a 10:00 P.M. curfew, a team psychiatrist, and no wives or girlfriends allowed. . . .

All of which, no matter how trifling or bizarre—or outright bogus—was more than news. And infinitely more than a game. It was life itself. It still is: politics, religion, theater, war, and sport—brought together, quadrennially (except when real war intervenes), in ninety-minute matches on fields of grass and mud. Dying men will themselves to stay alive for it; thousands have been killed in its name—6,000 alone in the 1970 "soccer war" between Honduras and

El Salvador, sparked by the on-field suicide of an eighteen-year-old girl. Defeat, especially for the great teams, is ignominy. Victory is the sweetest vindication a team, or nation, can know.

(So sweet sometimes it can only be explained divinely. Twenty years later almost to the day, in Mexico City in June of 1970, Brazil would again face the world-champion English—and would defeat them, improbably, on their way to winning the Cup. The week following, in Rio's *Jurnal dos Sportes,* under the headline "Jesus Defends Brazil," the victory would be described: "Whenever the ball flew toward our goal and a score [by the English] seemed inevitable, Jesus reached his foot out of the clouds and cleared the ball. . . ."

The report was dead earnest. To buttress it, a drawing by the newspaper's artist depicted the Almighty's foot.)

Of the four hundred reporters in Brazil those two weeks, only one was an American—Dent McSkimming, sportswriter for the *St. Louis Post-Dispatch.*

He was there, though, unofficially. Unable to convince his editors that the World Cup was news, he had put in for vacation and paid his own way down.

2

Among bookmakers in London the week before the game, the English were 3–1 to win the Cup.

Brazil, depending on whose odds you were quoting, ranged between 2–1 and 4–1. Italy, Spain, and Uruguay—the strength of the rest of the field—were bunched at odds of between 6–1 and 12–1. The Americans, when they were listed at all, were 500–1.

The war had muddied things. Italy had won the last two Cups—in 1934 and 1938—but had lost its best players in a plane crash (as well as losing the war) and was said to be demoralized and poorly trained. Spain was an enigma; it had had to labor in its opening match to beat the Americans, 3–1. Uruguay, which had won the Cup in 1930, had only token opposition (against Bolivia) in its opening pool and was all but impossible to judge.

The English were a known quantity. Or so it seemed. Since they'd returned to international play after the end of the war, they had dominated the continent. Two years before, they'd taken on a "Best of Europe" team—and humbled them, 6–1. Since then, they'd beaten the Italians, 4–0, in Turin, and the Portuguese, 10–0, in Lisbon, just weeks before. Their postwar record (prior to Cup play) was twenty-three wins, four losses, three ties.

They seemed unstoppable. Already, three days before—playing at what the press had called "half-pace"—they'd dispatched Chile, 2–0. Two days from now, following the formality of today's match against the United States, they would face Spain, the last and strongest of the four teams in Pool B.

On the strength of these three victories, they would move on to the medal round, at the end of which, if all went as presumed, they would finally meet Brazil. That game would take place in mid-July, in Rio's magnificent, just-completed Maracana Stadium, with 200,000 in the stands.

The Americans were an afterthought. That would be the kindest way to put it. What they were, really, was a joke. The last time they'd qualified for World Cup play, in 1934, they'd lost to Italy, 7–1—with Benito Mussolini, in yachting cap and binoculars, looking on from the stands. More recently, in the 1948 Olympics, with several of the same players they would field today, they'd been disgraced again by the Italians, 9–0. Since then, they'd lost 11–0 to Norway, 5–0 to Northern Ireland, and 4–0 to Scotland.

Before beating and tying Cuba in a pair of games the summer before (and being routed by Mexico twice) to qualify—absurdly— for the World Cup trip to Brazil, the Americans had lost seven straight international matches by the combined score of 45–2.

Against the English, if both teams played to form, they would lose by eight to twelve goals.

But almost no one in America cared. Or even knew. Soccer in the United States in 1950 was a sport shared by two subcultures—played passively by one, passionately by the second—and ignored by most everyone else.

The passive players were the sons (and occasionally daughters) of the old-money rich, who played it on the tended fields of northeastern prep schools and colleges, in keeping with the British mold in which such schools were cast. The passionate players were as opposite as their play: second- and third-generation immigrants— German, Italian, Belgian, Spanish, Haitian, Portuguese, Irish, and

Scot—who played it on the streets and playgrounds of expatriate neighborhoods in cities from Los Angeles to New York.

A few of these, a very few, played "professionally" in big-city immigrant leagues, for twenty or thirty dollars a game and the chance of getting noticed by a European club scout. The best of the rest played for "sponsors"—dry cleaners, car dealers, florists, or funeral homes—on weekend afternoons, for sneakers and expenses and whatever few dollars might be left over from the gate.

But almost no one made a living at it. And there wasn't one among them who wouldn't have played for free.

"It was a different time. You had no money; you had no car; there were no TVs in those days. What else were you going to do? You played ball. You grew up playing ball—soccer, baseball, stickball, whatever. You went out there every day, to the playground, and you got yourself a game. . . .

"So when somebody came along who'd offer you some bucks— well hey, that was money in the bank."

Walter Bahr is sixty-nine today. He was twenty-three when he took the field at left-halfback against the English in Belo Horizonte. And just over ten, he guesses, when he played in his first official game: for the Lighthouse Boys' Club of Philadelphia (dues, one dollar a year), on a playground field in his neighborhood of Kensington—English, Irish, German, and Scot, textile workers and packers of fish—against a rival team of ten-year-olds.

But by that time, one way or another, he'd been kicking around balls close to half his life.

"We were playground players. Like the kids you see today, shooting baskets in any city park—only basketball, in those days, at least where I grew up, was still pretty much a Jewish sport.

"But it was the same idea. We had our own organization, our own leaders; we made up our own rules. You could go to any playground, ask any kid there, 'Hey, who are the best players you got?'—and he'd tell you. The kids knew, the kids always knew. . . .

"If you were no good, it was, 'Hey, you're out, Smitty, we don't need you.' Or maybe you'd be fetching balls or [in baseball season] playing in deep right field. Either way, you weren't wanted and you knew it. So you got better. Either that, or you got out."

Walter Bahr, in 1950, was earning $2,400 a year as a phys ed teacher at John Paul Jones Junior High. And another $25 every Sunday, at halfback for the Philadelphia Nationals in the American Soccer League.

Across from him, at right-half that day in Brazil, was Ed McIlenny, also from Philadelphia, the only full-time pro on the team. Between them at center-half was Charley Columbo from St. Louis, a clerk in a meatpacking plant.

The fullbacks were Harry Keough, a St. Louis mailman, whose biggest payday on a soccer field—still to come—would be two hundred dollars for a forty-game season with the Kutis Funeral Home; and Joe Maca, who stripped wallpaper on Long Island for a decorating firm.

The center-forward, Joe Gaetjens, washed dishes in New York. His fellow attackmen were an unemployed jobber, a second mailman (also from St. Louis), a knitting machinist, and a sheet stacker at Continental Can.

Behind them all, defending goal, was Frank Borghi, a former minor-league catcher for a St. Louis farm team who now drove hearses for his uncle's funeral home.

Four were Italian, two Portuguese. The others were Belgian, Irish, German, Haitian, and Scot. They'd been winnowed through a season of low-budget tryouts—in Los Angeles, St. Louis, Chicago, and New York—then culled from the finalists, in a game of East versus West, in St. Louis just two months before.

It was the job of the U.S. Soccer Federation to field a national team. The federation's president was a man named Walter Giesler—who, when he chose to, served also as its scout. Giesler lived in St. Louis, as would six of the fifteen players (including substitutes) the federation would choose.

"I don't kid myself," says Harry Keough half a century later. "I wouldn't have made the team if I hadn't lived in town. So I owe that much to Mr. Giesler. But I like to think I proved him right."

. . .

Eight were U.S. citizens. The dishwasher, paper stripper, and soccer pro were not—and had probably lied (or been lied about) to get on the team. Most knew each other loosely—had played as opponents or on common teams—though the soccer pro and the dishwasher knew only the schoolteacher, and the paper stripper may have known no one at all.

Until their first scrimmage, in New York City just two weeks before, when they'd been beaten 5–0 by a club team from Istanbul, they had never before played together as a team. And after their next game—against Chile, the following Sunday in Recife—they never would again.

"A band of no-hopers," the *Belfast Telegram* would call them later, "drawn from many lands."

They probably deserved better than that. They could be dangerous—they could push even a good team to test itself. They'd proved it once already, against Spain.

They were young and tough, and, at least at the speed positions, very, very fast. They were not gentlemen. They hit hard—not always cleanly—and took hits without complaint. They weren't purists, either; they'd as soon win on grit as on finesse. And against a team of gentlemen-purists, this had to count as an edge.

They knew adversity. And they knew the game. They'd grown up playing it on neighborhood streets with inflated pig bladders for balls and shin guards of wadded magazines—taught by big brothers who'd learned it from neighborhood players, who'd been taught it by fathers, who'd known it from birth.

Their first memories were of the Depression. Joblines and breadlines and once-a-week meat. Their heroes, as boys, were ballplayers: Gehrig, DiMaggio, Ted Williams, Stan Musial, Johnny Mize. Their playtimes were stolen. Their greatest treasure was a four-dollar Spalding glove.

"As a kid back then," says Walter Bahr, "you didn't have a lot. Mashed potatoes and stewed tomatoes, that was dinner most nights. But you had your games. You always had your games."

. . .

Depression memories, told by one who has lived them to one who has not, seem a lot like Depression glass—puzzling, odd-colored, almost doleful in the sense they give off. But striking in their oddness, even beautiful sometimes.

"I remember this one time. I'll never forget it, it kind of changed the way I looked at things. I was thirteen, fourteen, something like that, having dinner at this friend of mine's house. Tommy Oliver. His parents were Scottish, first-generation, he was a good athlete, we were in school together at the time. . . .

"And the way things worked in those days, with most of the kids I knew—it was just sort of assumed that you'd quit school at sixteen and go to work. Nobody thought much about it; that's just the way things were. Tommy quit a couple years later. But we were in school together then. . . .

"Anyway, we're sitting down to dinner at his house, and there's this plate of porkchops on the table. The only thing was—and I didn't know it till it happened, it sort of took me back—you only got a porkchop if you worked.

"That was the rule. The porkchops went to the workers, nobody else. Didn't matter who you were, how old you were. Tommy didn't get a porkchop, I didn't get a porkchop. I've always remembered that."

There is a photo in an old news clipping, taken in 1953 before an exhibition game between England and the United States. But it could as easily be three years earlier, before the game in Brazil.

Walter Bahr, the U.S. team captain, is shaking hands with Billy Wright, the captain of the English team. Both players are looking at the camera, as are all three stripe-shirted referees, who stand a foot or two behind. Wright and the refs are smiling blankly—an empty-eyed, pregame publicity smile.

Bahr is not smiling. His lips are closed, and pressed tight.

Wright is the picture of jauntiness. The taller of the two by several inches, he poses almost languidly—body tipped slightly toward the camera, shoulders forward, right arm fully stretched. Bahr seems a mannequin: stiff, wide-eyed, expressionless, erect. His left arm is thrust awkwardly behind him, as though to hide some deformity to his hand. He looks ready to bolt.

They could be a pair of dogs in a show ring. Same age and coloring, identically groomed and clipped. But the larger one is a purebred, raised on meat to win ribbons, as comfortable in the ring as in bed. The other is a street dog—skittish, narrow-eyed, habitually hungry—now gussied up for the day.

The purebred would win on style points. A street fight could go either way.

3

We had this game, as kids," Gino Pariani, the sheet stacker, remembers. "We called it Indian Rubber Ball. I can't remember where the name came from. . . .

"The width of the street was our field—there weren't a lot of cars back then. You'd have an infielder and two outfielders, and the idea was to bat the ball through the infield without it being caught. Two fouls and you were out. We used bricks to mark the foul lines. Four hits in one inning was a run."

Gino Pariani was twenty-two, a husband of three days, when he flew out of St. Louis for New York City the morning of June 17. Eight days later, a hemisphere away, he had scored the only U.S. goal against Spain.

And now, four days after that and five hundred miles farther north, he lined up at right-inside, between the dishwasher and the second mailman, in a futile cause against the inventors of the game.

He is sixty-eight today. And, except for the hair, which has gone to slate gray from bushy black, he looks uncannily the same as the dark, Italianate young man with the hooded eyes who peers out at you from the center of the front row of the 1950 U.S. team photo. Tanned, eagle-featured, and still as wiry as a sprinter, he is the picture of the athlete who has held on past his time.

Not that he is youthful—he looks every bit his age—but there is a grittiness about him, a sense of toughness stored deep, that you can tell he will take to his grave.

He smiles thinly and not often, but with a softness that could not be staged. His words are few—he is not a natural talker—and seem somehow hurried: the chopped, impatient rhythms of a man for whom words have never carried much weight. Everything about him seems unpolished, and utterly without guile. He is the sort of man you meet rarely, a man you instinctively trust.

"Everyday after school, till maybe eight, nine o'clock at night, you'd be out there playing ball in the street—you call 'em streets today; it was more like just the neighborhood, really. You could go from one block, there'd be this whole bunch of your friends—family, friends, the two was pretty much the same.

"Next corner, same thing. You go outside your house, and just on that one street, you got enough for two nine-man softball teams. . . ."

He grew up on Daggett Avenue in St. Louis, in a neighborhood known in those days as Dago Hill, the son of Giovanni Pariani, born in 1896 in Castano Primo just west of Milan, who had left home at seventeen, settled in St. Louis, married an Italian, and gone to work in a brickyard at $1.80 a day. He retired at sixty-six and was dead three years later.

"He nothing but worked," says his youngest son today.

As a boy, after school, young Gino pressed rugs and steamed mattresses for Lungstras Laundry. And kept one, sometimes none, of the ten dollars he earned every week. Still, unlike his older brother, to whom the heavier burden fell—born six years sooner, a thirteen-year-old in harsher times, Angelo rose every morning in the darkness to deliver blocks of ice—Gino stayed in school until he finished. And his evenings and weekends were his own.

"My brother, he more or less spent all his time working; I never really knew him too well. But I had a cousin, Mike Montani—we always just called him 'Tusky,' though. He was ten, maybe twelve years older than me; he used to play ball for this team they called the Hawks.

"And on Saturdays usually, when they'd be working out, I'd go down there to the park and fetch balls—I was just this little kid—and kick around, and watch, and in general just sort of hang out. . . .

"And so it got to, after a while, if they was short a guy or something, Tusky or one of 'em would say, 'Hey, Gino, you wanna fill in?'

"And that was how you learned. You learned by watching, and waiting, and just being there and hangin' out."

It can be a sad thing to listen to a nearly old man recall the street games of his youth. So often, there is an edge of longing, of wistfulness for a time that grows fuller in remembering, of unmet promise and long-dead dreams.

"The good days," "my younger days," "I remember the day"—only you know, and he knows, that the days were never so good, or so memorable, that he never hit .300 or scored the winning goal. Or that—if he did, or they were—life since has been fallow, and the only joy left is in reprise.

It is not so with these men. Not even a little, not even with one. And there are five today still living, of the eleven who took the field in Brazil:

Gino Pariani and Walter Bahr. Frank Borghi, the hearse-driving goalkeeper. Harry Keough, the fullback from St. Louis who carried the mail. And John ("Clarkie") Sousa, left-inside, a Portuguese knitting machinist and the strongest dribbler on the team.

Their average age today is a month over seventy. All five are grandfathers; all five still married, each to his original bride. None are poor, or even struggling. Or weak-brained, or alcoholic, or frail. There isn't one who couldn't touch his toes, or fling his grandkids, or sit for an hour over a puzzle, or carry a pack three miles.

They are jokers too, every one. They laugh and party, and play golf and bocce, and attend reunions—and funerals—and their grandkids' fourth-grade plays. Their wives are pretty; their homes are paid for, well-tended, and bright. Their sons and daughters live close by, do well, and bring joy.

As athletes, they were brilliant but unknown. They played for pittances, in front of small crowds in rickety bleachers on rented playground fields. The loudest cheers they ever heard were from 30,000 Brazilians who would never know their names. They were heroes to their little brothers, if they were ever heroes at all.

None of this troubles them. On a recent weekend afternoon in St. Louis, around a table in Janet and Gino Pariani's kitchen, the former U.S. right-inside and his old teammate Harry Keough drink Cokes and answer questions, their eyes all the while on the living room TV—where the current crop of U.S. players are subduing Mexico by a margin that grows as they watch.

On the field for the United States this day are Alexei Lalas and Cobi Jones, the team's two biggest names. Between them, probably, in endorsements alone, they earn more in a single year playing soccer than the eleven-man 1950 U.S. team, combined, earned through their careers.

Do they ever wish they'd been born a half century later?

"Hell, no—why?" says Pariani.

"More power to 'em," says Keough.

And that is all, for the time being, that either one has to say.

A minute or two later, Lalas takes a vicious elbow to the head from a Mexican at midfield. The crowd groans; Lalas falls to the ground. The camera goes in tight. Lalas grimaces, then sneers, then gets up slowly—the camera still on him—and hobbles after play.

"But hey, Harry," his old friend says now, "I'll bet we had more fun."

4

They arrived by bus at the stadium an hour before game time. Eleven starters, three substitutes (though substitutions, in those days, were not allowed), and Bill Jeffrey, their just-appointed coach—a bald, round-faced, middle-aged Scotsman with a temperate manner and a perpetual half smile.

Jeffrey, the former coach of several second-level English teams—and then the coach at Penn State—was openly unimpressed with the prospects of his team.

"We have no chance," he told a British reporter. "Do the best you can" is the only advice any player can recall.

"He didn't have the time to do much coaching," says Walter Bahr today. "And he was smart enough not to try."

They were a loose group. Eleven working men in their twenties on vacation in Brazil—with nothing to prove, nothing to lose, five dollars a day in meal money and a hundred dollars a week to spend. If they'd been anyone else but who they were (or the English had been anything less), they might have been seen as dangerous, or at least worth measuring a bit.

16

But they weren't. And the notion of a Walter Winterbottom, for eighteen years the English coach, warning his players before a World Cup match, "Watch out for the Americans," (though it would be reported, later, that he had tried) was more than preposterous. Like telling a world-class swimmer to be sure and strap on his life vest before going into the deep end of the pool.

And so, ignored, the eleven young men carried on. And had not, so far, disgraced themselves.

Four days earlier in Curitiba, as a six-goal underdog against Spain, they had taken a 1–0 lead in the twenty-third minute, on a goal by Gino Pariani, then held it for fifty minutes more, before finally yielding, 3–1. The Spanish had blamed themselves. The press, and the bookies, had downgraded Spain. The odds on the Americans hadn't moved.

"We were probably better than they gave us credit for," Walter Bahr says today. "We couldn't match [England's] talent, but the chemistry was right."

Soccer, Bahr is fond of explaining, is "a game of pairs, playing together." When the pairs match well, the chemistry is right. And with the right chemistry, he says, "and your share of the breaks, a lot of good can happen."

To hear him tell it, it sounds almost more like dance than sport—though perhaps, to his ears, that distinction would seem moot. A weekend pro for twenty-three years, a coach for close to forty (he retired from Penn State, as head soccer coach, in 1988), and married half a century to a teacher of dance, he is a qualified spokesman for the rhythms and pairings of sport.

And looking today at that U.S. eleven, from the hindsight of nearly fifty years, he rates them as a well-paired group:

On the left-front line, Ed and Clarkie Sousa (no relation), both Portuguese, both from Fall River, Massachusetts, former teammates for Ponta del Gados: "Tough, fast, excellent ball handlers—especially Clarkie. Great stamina. They played off each other well. . . ."

On the right front, Gino Pariani and Frank ("Peewee") Wallace—longtime friends, St. Louis natives, teammates for the Schumaker Funeral Home: "Aggressive, good shooters, always a threat. Peewee had great foot speed; Gino was small but tough—a playmaker. A natural pairing. Maybe the best matchup we had. . . ."

The outside halfbacks, Ed McIlenny and Bahr himself, both twenty-five-dollar-a-game players for the Philadelphia Nationals of the American Soccer League: "Ed had incredible talent. He'd intercept passes as though they'd been meant for him—he had such a nose for the ball. My strength was ball control; his was timing and speed. We were a strong defensive pair. . . ."

The fullbacks, Joe Maca and Harry Keough: "They'd never played together, but they matched up well. Similar-type players. Both good ball handlers, which is unusual for defensive backs. Not huge speed, but they knew how to shorten the field."

And the trio of loners, the unpaired three.

Joe Gaetjens at center-forward: "athletic, acrobatic, unpredictable, a free spirit. He was perfect for the role."

Charley Columbo—also called "Lefty," also called "Gloves"—at center-half: "Hard, tough, probably the toughest player we had" (some would say the dirtiest). "The perfect stopper—he broke up everything in the middle of the field. He made up in toughness what he lacked in pure skill. The guy would do anything to win."

And in the goalmouth, Frank Borghi, former catcher and .275 hitter with the Class D Carthage Cardinals of the KOM League, now goalie for Joe Simpkins Ford: "Terrific hands, great instincts, great anticipation. And he could throw the ball a mile."

They'd had far too little sleep. Since they'd flown out of New York City on a midnight flight eleven days before—following a banquet at the Waldorf with members of the English team—they'd spent eighteen hours in six airports in three countries (twelve hours, delayed by engine troubles, in San Juan alone), and at least thirty more hours in the air. They had practiced four times, played one game, and slept in five different hotels.

There is no counting how many bars they'd visited. Joe Gaetjens claimed twelve in Rio, in one night alone. So when they showed up at the stadium the morning of the twenty-ninth, they were a sorry-looking group.

"The Americans came strolling into the dressing rooms in Belo Horizonte, surely the strangest team ever to [be seen] at a World

Cup," the *Belfast Telegram* would report. "Some wore Stetsons, some smoked big cigars, and some were still in the happy, early stages of hangovers. . . ."

Joe Gaetjens yawned and shuffled, only barely awake. An hour earlier, dragged from his bed by Harry Keough, he had seemed more dead than alive. But this, for Gaetjens, was nothing new.

"Joe always swore he played better if he partied—you know, caroused a little—the night before a game," Harry Keough remembers. "He claimed it kept him looser, said he stiffened up with too much sleep.

"And hey, with the things that guy could do on the field, who was going to tell him what time to go to bed?"

Joe Gaetjens was a strange bird. A twenty-six-year-old New York City dishwasher, the son of a Haitian mother and Belgian father, he had left Haiti at twenty-two to study accounting—which he was doing still, at Columbia University, part-time. He played his soccer for the Brook-Hattan Galicia, a semipro club in the American league.

No one on the team knew much about him. Until two months earlier, at the Cup tryouts in St. Louis, only Walter Bahr had ever seen him play.

Even today, they can't agree on what to call him: "quirky," "strange," "eccentric," "loosey-goosey," a "free spirit"—though all these tell you, really, is that he wasn't much like any of them. From all reports, he smiled a lot (in the 1950 team photo, he is the only player with anything resembling a smile), sometimes for reasons that no one but he could understand.

He had strange tastes and odd fixations—such as hating (this from Harry Keough) to wear his socks rolled up, or to wear jerseys that were any tighter than tents. "He'd say to me, 'Harry, Harry, they want me to—' And I'd say, 'Don't worry about it, Joe, they'll never notice. Just wait till the game starts, then let the socks fall down.' And he would. Then the next thing you know, he'd have his jersey ripped halfway down the front."

He played soccer, though, as if the world were ending—and its deliverance depended only on him. He did things with his body, to hear his teammates tell it, that no one but he would have tried: up and around larger players, kamikaze blocks and slides, headlong dives at balls a giraffe couldn't reach.

"I saw him for the first time in St. Louis," says Keough. "I thought he was different, a little crazy, I wasn't sure just what to think. But then Walter took me aside, and he told me, 'Harry,' he said, 'I've seen this guy play. He's a little nuts, a little cuckoo; you call it whatever you want. But he makes some of the most uncanny goals you've ever seen in your life.'"

Joe Gaetjens was light-skinned for a Haitian, though he could probably have been taken for black. "A half-Negro dishwasher," the 1950 U.S. papers might have called him—straightforwardly, as a distinction of fact—if more than one writer had been covering the game.

It was still that time in America. Jackie Robinson, the best in baseball three years after breaking the color line, was still (depending on your sources) the "Negro Dodger" or "that nigger who ruined the game." The Rosenbergs, to millions, were Jews before they were traitors. Joe McCarthy was gaining credence by the day.

And in St. Louis, the highest point of land in the city, where much of the nation's best soccer was played, was still known, semiofficially, as Dago Hill.

While on the field in Belo Horizonte, eleven young Americans— including four dagos—the sons of fathers from seven lands, lined up in the colors of their country to play a game that belonged to every country but theirs.

5

The English wore royal blue, short-sleeved jerseys over white shorts. The Americans wore white over blue—some short sleeves, some long—with a broad red stripe running diagonally the length of their chests.

The English were fair-skinned, lanky, and well barbered. A wholesome, very British lot. The Americans were fair, swarthy, negroid; handsome and snout-nosed; lean, stocky, broad-shouldered, slope-shouldered, bushy-haired, fuzzy-haired, and bald.

The bald one was the best dribbler, the snout-nose made the hardest hits. The fuzzy-haired goalkeeper had hands like pressed hams, a size-fourteen shoe, and an arm that could send a ball half the field.

These were the key three: Clarkie Sousa, Charley Columbo, Frank Borghi—who, even more than the others, if there were to be any miracles in Belo Horizonte that day, would have to manufacture the game of their lives.

Sousa was the playmaker, the ball-control artist, the only man on the team with the foot-touch to challenge the Brits. If Gaetjens or

Pariani were to have any chance at the English goal, it would likely be Sousa who would bring them in range.

"Gloves" Columbo was the street fighter; his trademark, a pair of stained leather boxing mittens (today on display in the U.S. Soccer Hall of Fame), which he never explained, never used for anything in particular, and never removed on the field. ("I just like them," he had told a reporter once.) Scrappy, fearless, relentless, foulmouthed, intimidating—and as dirty as he needed to be—there was nothing he wouldn't do to strip a man from the ball. ("He would have crippled his grandmother," says Walter Bahr today.) He was a poise tester. The English were known for their poise. If he could break it, even stretch it, there was no telling what walls might come down.

Borghi was just Borghi—the goalkeeper, the last man in the way. And against the English, no matter how well or bravely his defensive backs played, he was sure to take the battering of his life. Thirty shots—unscreened, unimpeded—were not unlikely that day.

The English won the coin toss. Roy Bentley, center-forward, tapped back to Billy Wright at wing-half. And the dominance, and stupefaction, began. . . .

Wright had expected it. He trapped it easily, placed it between his feet, and waited. For nothing in particular—perhaps for the Americans to be fools enough to move.

No one moved. The ball sat, as though a bird fallen from the sky, delivered dead between his feet. He nudged it—left foot, right foot, left, right, left. A pantomime of dribbling. The ball rolled over, then back, going nowhere. All ten forwards frissoned. No one moved.

A dozen or more times he did this. Left nudge, right nudge . . .

Until came the nudge, just as forceless, with just as little leg, that was a pass instead—forward ten yards, bullet-straight, to Tom Finney at outside-right.

So began a show of mastery, so precise yet simple it seemed almost exotic. The crowd, with each half minute, grew quieter. By the end of three minutes, there was no sound at all from the stands. They were an audience now.

. . .

Finney was one of England's greats. Slight, baby-faced, two-footed and agile, midway through a twelve-year, thirty-goal career (a record at the time)—he took the ball now, a yard inside the right touchline, pivoted left to head off Eddie Sousa coming fast from upfield, then dribbled laterally, toward center, roughly along the midfield line. The field moved with him, Sousa on his right shoulder, Joe Gaetjens charging from his front.

He pulled up—a yard inside the center circle, two yards, perhaps less, inside the U.S. zone. Three of the five U.S. forwards now ringed him; the halfbacks were pulled tight behind.

Nothing much had happened. Bentley to Wright to Finney, the ball ahead two yards. But this—always, for decades now—had been the English game: slow the pace, tighten the field, let the match go sluggish. Then strike as best you can. European soccer, unlike U.S. football, has never been a sport that gulps yards.

Finney, his upfield lanes stoppered, passed cross-field to Bentley—at the perimeter of the circle, six yards farther left. Charley ("Lay in the Weeds") Columbo closed on Bentley like a truck.

He should have closed on the ball. He might have had it, but that was never his way. Bentley saw him coming. He waited, then stepped aside. Columbo went past; the ball, for half an instant, rolled free. . . .

It was Mortensen's turn now. Stanley Mortensen, the fastest player on the English side, perhaps (probably) the fastest on the field—only Peewee Wallace would have given him a race—circled quickly, scooped the ball off the back-left half of the center circle, turned, and headed like a rabbit upfield.

He crossed the half-line at a dead run, Bentley and left-wing Jimmy Mullen alongside. Gaetjens and Wallace closed fast from the right; Columbo was a yard or two behind. But for those twelve or fifteen sprinted steps, Mortensen—three years later, in his finest moment, the only man in history ever to score a hat trick at the Wembley Cup final—was as good as alone on the field.

．　．　．

He took it deep—but couldn't cut inside. The United States had built a wall there: Bahr, Keough, Pariani, with Columbo dogging from behind. The ball, now twenty yards left of center, thirty yards out from goal, became less a threat with every stride.

He took it deeper: another twelve yards, just short of the penalty line. But still he couldn't cut in. He pulled up. The defense clotted tighter. He was outmanned, badly boxed. He seemed certain to lose the ball.

He shot, left to right—you would have said in surrender, but the ball found a hole: straight as a plumb line through the knot of defenders, barely leaving the ground, never touching a foot—a perfect, brilliant, twenty-yard cross.

Two yards deep in the penalty zone, it found the foot of Roy Bentley—fifteen yards from the goalmouth, with only Frank Borghi to beat.

Bentley kicked: a left-footed bullet toward the far right corner, twelve inches off the grass.

Borghi dove—and was still in the air when the ball caromed off the post—back a full yard from his fingers, and careened, still aloft, out of bounds.

The crowd was still. The game was ninety seconds old. Half the English side had handled the ball: four passes, five possessions, one clean shot. No U.S. toe had yet touched it.

Things got no better. By twelve minutes into the game, the English had had six clear shots. Two, like the first, came off crosses into the penalty zone; a third was off a corner kick. But however they happened, all six were much the same—the codas of compact, rhythmical, half-team pass drills, linking the attackers in polygons of shifting shapes. Sometimes lateral, more often downfield, but always purposeful and economic, and as undivinable as gusts of wind.

"The man with the ball"—Hubert Vogelsinger would write, twenty years later, of the Hungarian national team—"was like a stone thrown into water, because around him, but not too near, were a cluster of players like outgoing ripples in a water splash. Each time the ball moved around the field, a new set of ripples was created."

The Americans seemed transfixed. They dove; they charged; they pursued. They threw their bodies into tackles. But they almost never moved ahead. Twice during those twelve minutes, they gained control—and just as quickly, lost it. Unable to set up, to break clear of the English players marking them, or to achieve any semblance of purpose or wile, they passed errantly, sometimes wildly, as skittish and random seeming as a school of panicked fish.

Their possession time couldn't have totaled thirty seconds. Only once, and only briefly, did they make it within range of the English goal—at which point Peewee Wallace delivered a shot to English fullback Alf Ramsey, on a line as straight as a length of stretched rope.

But the English, to save themselves, couldn't score. Two shots already had caromed off the post. A third—by Mortensen, an all but certain goal, shot from ten yards out with Borghi drawn hopelessly wide—sailed inches over the bar. It was the first of a dozen overkicks the press, and the English, would later blame on the grass.

Borghi was magnificent. Once, against a header by inside-left Wilf Mannion from fifteen yards out, he dove diagonally almost the length of the goal, deflecting the ball over the top of the net with what couldn't have been more than a fingertip, impossibly stretched.

Another time, leaping to catch a ball that was dropping vertically into a scrum of players a yard in front of his net, he towered so high over the highest of them that he appears—in the photo that survives of that moment—to be a man among dwarfs.

It was nearly as remarkable, in the long view of things, that Frank Borghi was there at all. As a boy, he'd had no talent for soccer. He was long-limbed and gangly; his feet were too big. It just wasn't his game.

"I always loved to run, I loved kicking the ball around and all that, but I never really had the skills. I couldn't handle the ball the way Harry [Keough] could. I couldn't trap it or pass it; I couldn't keep it on my toes. . . ."

His real love was baseball. At Macklind Field in St. Louis, as a twelve-year-old on Saturday afternoons—"with sometimes twelve, fourteen guys on a side"—then later with the Lefty Lyfields of the

American Legion League, he had played third base and shortstop, and learned early that he had far more promise with a glove and bat than he would ever have with his feet.

"Baseball, the hitting, the catching—the game just came natural to me."

Had he lived anywhere else but St. Louis, or in any other time, he might never have played soccer again. But the city, in those years, was the capital of the sport in America. A million fans a year attended hundreds of matches at a dozen parks and fields. The rivalries were ethnic and religious—the Germans, the Spanish, the Irish of Kerry Patch, the Italians of Little Italy and Dago Hill—the sons of urban Catholic immigrants, playing often under the banner of a St. Ambrose or an Our Lady of Hope, slugging out their hatreds and escaping their trials in ninety-minute, mostly bloodless wars.

"In the palmy days of yore, when order reigned over innocent games"—Frank Deford would write, of immigrant-athletes, in *Sports Illustrated* forty years later—"sport was uplifting, and a glorious celebration, like the Mass. Sport and the church both stood for authority. . . . Heroes were larger than life, canonized as athletic saints. . . ."

So Frank Borghi learned soccer. And over time, he came to learn his role.

"The one thing I could always do, that I knew I could do, was catch a ball. I had that confidence in my hands. I never learned the fundamentals; I was never fancy like some of the keepers you see today. But I knew two things. . . .

"I could field the ball like a shortstop, that was the first. And the other, the one they tell you when you're just starting out—'Sonny, keep your eye on the ball.'"

He is a big man. Not fat at all—there's not a trace of fat on him—just big. Everything about him is big. His hand swallows yours when he shakes it; his feet could be pontoons. He is large-headed, long-necked, long striding. The power in his grip—he is seventy-one years old—would be shocking from a man half his age.

"Gentle giant" could have been coined to describe him. He blushes almost constantly, at every suggestion of praise; he speaks slowly, occasionally with what seems a stammer. He extols everyone but himself.

His smile is enormous and nearly permanent. But almost sad sometimes in the humility it betrays. It is impossible to imagine that he has ever in his life raised his voice.

He played, over the years—between baseball and soccer, between junior and senior leagues—for too many teams to keep straight: the Ravens, the Lefty Lyfields, St. Ambrose parish, the Schumacker Funeral Home; Correnti Cleaners, the Carondelet Sunday Morning Club, Patterson Ford, Simpkins Ford, the Forty-and-Eight.

Most have long since disbanded, their sponsors bankrupt, mergered, or dead. But they remain, nearly all of them, in the broken-covered scrapbook he still keeps—sixty-odd pages of yellowed newsclips he pulls out from a bottom drawer.

> "Simpkins Heavy Choice to Reach Western Final"
> "Borghi a Sensation in Goal"
> "St. Ambrose Edged, 2–1, in Late Going"
> "Borghi Voted Most Valuable"
> "Simpkins Routs Diamonds, 9–0"
> "Borghi: Three Home Runs in Three Times at Bat"

And a hundred others at least, many with photos. Borghi, leaping high—a full head above any player near him—for a near-impossible save. A teammate or opponent wrenching feet-first or headlong into an all-important, decades-forgotten, goal-saving tackle-slide. The city-champion Simpkins Ford, mugging for the 1952 team shot. ("I remember that game—that game was a war. . . ." "That guy there—he had a foot on him you wouldn't believe. . . ." "This guy, he used to play for Schumacker; he died a couple years back. . . .")

He hasn't looked at the album in years. He thumbs through it now, chuckling, recalling, once in a while shaking his head. It no longer seems precious to him—more relic now than treasure. He is happy to loan it, he says. ("Take it. Go ahead, take it. Get it back whenever you can.")

*   *   *

His father died when he was fifteen. He quit school a year later—in 1941, the same year his Dago Hill neighbor, Yogi Berra, was signed by the New York Yankees—to work as a bundle dropper for the Famous and Barr Department Store. The work wasn't always regular.

"We used to go down there to Spring Avenue, and just sit down in front of the store, and the bosses would come out and they'd say, 'This route needs a helper' or 'That route needs a helper,' and you'd go with 'em, and just do like they said."

On weekends, at the time, he played in goal for the Schumacker Funeral Home; or—the other half year—at third base for the Lefty Lyfields.

"I remember this one game. A big game, against the Johnny Brocks in Sportsmen's Park. And Yogi, he was playing for the Brocks at the time—along with Joe Garagiola"—who would be drafted six months later by the St. Louis Cardinals, bat .316 in the 1946 World Series, then make his name as host of the *Today* show.

"And Yogi, he hits this drive to right-center, takes off for second, and beats the throw from the field. . . .

"Well, in the paper the next morning, they had the picture. And the headline—whaddaya s'pose it said? 'Just Like Big Leaguers.' Isn't that somethin'? 'Just Like Big Leaguers.' I still got that paper somewhere."

Yogi Berra and Joe Garagiola grew up as neighbors on Elizabeth Avenue, four blocks from Frank Borghi's uncle's funeral home. Both dropped out of school early; both were signed to major-league contracts before they were seventeen—a tonic to the dreams of every boy on Dago Hill.

"Yogi was good. I'm not sayin' I was better, but I always felt that I could have made it up there. I had good hands, and I batted pretty good. But there was a lotta talent around in those days. And in the end, like they say, you never really can tell."

He turned eighteen in April of 1943. And went to war. Before his twentieth birthday, he would serve—as a combat medic with the Ninth Infantry Division—in the Ardennes Forest, on Utah Beach in the Normandy campaign (where he would leave his poncho with a dying German soldier: "an older gentleman; he kind of smiled at me, like he appreciated it, but I had to move on"), in Germany, and in southern France. He would win a Purple Heart and a Bronze Star, rise to the rank of staff sergeant, and suffer shell shock from German artillery in a trench in the north of France.

"I was a kid; I was scared. Every shell comes, you think it's gonna be yours."

He returned home, the war over, in the late summer of 1945. His hearse-driving job was waiting. And for that fall and winter and part of the next spring, he ferried bodies, filled in at third base for the Carondelet Sunday Morning Club, and dickered endlessly with his uncle and mother about the direction his future would take.

"They wanted to send me to embalming school. I didn't want to be an embalmer, it wasn't how I saw my life."

In mid-March of 1946, a man named Joe Mathes, a scout for the St. Louis Cardinals farm system, arrived at the Borghi family home. He carried with him a check for $100—"a bonus, you can cash it in the morning"—an unsigned contract, and the offer of $125 a month.

Twenty days later, on a red-dirt field in Carthage, Missouri, with 350 in the stands, young Frank Borghi singled up the middle in his first at-bat as a pro.

He finished the 1946 season with a .275 average, eleven home runs, and forty runs batted in. He was moved up the next season: from Carthage to Jackson, Mississippi, from Class D to Class B—and moved over, to catcher from third base.

Those are treasured years today. He smiles often, sometimes sadly, as he recalls them, and can still summon the smallest things.

"We were playing for peanuts, traveling around in beat-up old buses; we slept usually three to a room. But they fed us pretty good, and there were always ways to make a buck. This one guy, Buzz Arbett, he played first base in Carthage, and drove the bus for an extra fifty bucks a month. . . .

"The crowds were small, but they loved us. They treated us like kings. In Carthage, if you got the winning hit in a game, the fans, they'd pass a hat—you might get fifteen, maybe twenty dollars. And if you hit the scoreboard on the fly—well then, you got yourself a free pair of pants."

Sometime between the 1947 and 1948 seasons, another scout came around. This one, as he recalls it, may have been from the Giants or Dodgers. But the memory is too painful to be fresh.

"My mother, she told him, 'My Frankie, he don't want to play ball no more'—only she didn't say it that nice. And he went away, and he didn't come back."

It was the only real dream he'd ever had. It was ended at twenty-two. He went back to school and back to driving hearses. He became a soccer player again—a year with Correnti Cleaners, nine years with Simpkins Ford. He won two national championships (in 1948 and 1952) and a lifetime's worth of teammate-friends. He played some fast-pitch softball in his thirties. He never played baseball again.

He became, after all, a mortician (though he never did learn to embalm) and is today the proprietor of the Calcaterra Funeral Home—founded by his uncle, Paul Calcaterra, in 1923—in the section of St. Louis now known simply as the Hill.

He is known locally as "the merry mortician." It is a job, he says, that grows harder with the years.

"It gets kinda personal. Anytime the phone rings, you know it's another friend gone. I buried Charley; I buried Peewee; I buried Bobby Annis (another old teammate, a backup on the 1950 World Cup squad) just last month."

In 1948, he met Rosemary Novara—a pretty, sharp-witted Sicilian with a room-lighting smile. Today, they have seven children, ten grandchildren. She keeps the books for the funeral home and plays bocce in a women's league Wednesday nights. Her smile is still radiant. They remain openly, playfully, in love.

It's hard to get him to say much about the Dodger scout his mother sent away. "I wish sometimes I'd given it an honest effort—say four, five years in the minors; it takes that long to make it, for most guys anyway. And things was going pretty good. It makes me sad when I think about it, so I don't think about it too much."

And then, in the very next breath: "Like I tell my wife, I might have made the big leagues and gotten rich and famous. But instead I met a girl—and I'm a happy man."

6

1st HALF
21:35

A t about the midpoint of the first half, the pace of play seemed to ease. The English, who by now had gotten off close to a dozen clean shots—all high or wide, or routinely, or remarkably, stopped—seemed suddenly at home with their dominance, no longer impatient for a score.

"It was as though," Harry Keough would say later, "they finally found their range. They knew they couldn't keep hitting the post forever—and we certainly weren't giving them any scare. Sooner or later, I guess they figured, the ball was going to go in."

"Like a veteran boxer stalking his novice opponent"—a torn, unattributed, and barely legible newsclip in Frank Borghi's old scrapbook reads—"the English seemed patiently to be measuring their foe. The Yanks were courageous, but altogether without punch. The English passed sharply, held possession, and waited for their chance."

It was midafternoon. The temperature on the field was just short of eighty, about right for early winter in Brazil. There was no wind to speak of, and next to no clouds—a desultory day. In the stands, where the mood by now was restive, some of the men drank from bottles of beer. Below them, defending the English goal, fair-haired Bert Williams, alone and untested, fanned his arms to keep from growing stiff.

The Americans had yet to threaten. Several times, they had crossed the half-line; each time, as though paralyzed by their success, they had overshot, been stripped of the ball, or passed it, seeming aimless, away. Their only real shot—by Peewee Wallace, from twenty yards out—had been too high and wide to cause Bert Williams to even move a step.

But inside their own half, they were as scrappy as mongrel dogs. Finesse was not an issue. They charged every dribbler, challenged for every free ball. The fullbacks, Keough and Maca, like movable foothills to the right and left of Borghi's goal, forced attackers wide to the corners, dogged them, pestered them, blocked their passes, and tangled their feet.

The crowd, who disdained artlessness but admired above all else an underdog's grit, began—at first tamely—to respond.

Charley Columbo was a wrecking machine. His mark, as center-half, was English striker Roy Bentley—though strict defensive coverage was never Columbo's game. He bullied, really, more than covered; there was nothing defensive in anything he did. He was tall and tough, and mean looking. And he wore those gloves. There was no artistry about him. His style was to dominate through fear.

From the opening moments, he took on Bentley, who was not a small man. But size was never an issue with Columbo; he was a rib gouger, a head butter, a kneer of groins. He hit you when you weren't looking, from sideways or behind—an instant later, he was ten yards downfield.

Four days before, in the game against the Spanish, he'd made a bet with backup goalie Gino Gard. If he could hold Spain's center-forward scoreless, Gard would pick up the tab for a night's worth of beers; if the center-forward scored, it would be Columbo's night to buy. The bet, as much as the game, was the talk of the team that week.

"He was all over the guy, all game long," as Keough recounts it.

"He was holding him, he was kicking him, insulting him any way he could—'You stink, you son of a bitch, *stupido, stupido,* I could cover you in a wheelchair'—that's the sort of stuff he said. And a minute or so before the end of the game, the guy, he still hasn't scored. . . .

"Then, with maybe forty-five seconds to go, the son of a bitch, he headed one in. And Charley, he takes off his gloves, and he throws them in the air—I maybe never saw him so mad. . . .

"And the guy, he comes up to Charley, he gets right in his face, and he says, *'Pa tu madre'*—'For your mother'—and he runs off down the field."

Only once in the first thirty minutes did Columbo manage to put Bentley in the dirt—with a blindsided foot-tackle that took his legs out from under him as cleanly as if they'd been severed at the knees. But he dogged him ceaselessly: rib-digs, shoulder-butts, rear-end charges that had nothing to do with the ball. Bentley cursed him at every whistle. Columbo sneered, spat, and called him gutter names.

Opinion is divided where Charley Columbo is concerned. Walter Bahr and Harry Keough will tell you he played outside the rules; neither one, fifty years later, has very much good to say. Gino Pariani, who knew him the longest and best—they were baseball opponents, as kids in the 1930s, and soccer teammates for three decades after that—rates him as an "incredible competitor" who won games "just by his presence on the field."

Frank Borghi, who knew him nearly as long but would be hard-pressed to speak ill of the devil himself, says simply: "Charley played to win. And he mostly always did."

Not one of them—not anyone at all—would dispute that. It didn't matter what the game was; if winning was your only object, Charley Columbo was the first guy you wanted on your side.

"Charley's up there at the plate," says Keough, who may be the least of his fans, "and the count, let's say, is three-and-oh. The pitcher goes into his windup—and just at that second, Charley, he tosses down his bat and starts jogging toward first base. . . .

"Well, he's maybe five yards down the first-base line when the ball crosses the plate, and the umpire yells, 'Strike One!' And Charley—who hasn't even seen the ball—he stops in his tracks and stares at the guy. 'What's that?' he says, and his eyes go all buggy and wide. 'You calling that thing a strike?'

"That was Charley for you. There wasn't much he wouldn't do to give himself an edge."

Gino Pariani may have been the best friend he had. They were devoted to each other—both scrappy and guileless, both the sons of Dago Hill fathers who smelted firebricks for a living at $2.40 a day. Neither one had much use for whiners.

"A lotta people will tell you Charley played dirty, that he took cheap shots and all. Well, lemme tell you something. The people who say that? They never saw the guy in the shower after the game; they never saw the bruises up and down his legs. Ugly, black-and-blue stuff from his knees on down.

"They seen that, maybe they'd shut up. But they never knew—'cause Charley, he never bitched. He took his hits; he got up like nothing had happened. But you see him in the shower, you knew. The guy was in some pain. . . .

"Cheap shots, hell. He took as good as he gave. He was a classy guy, a hard-nosed player. I was proud to play with him."

Columbo, through the late 1940s and 1950s, played at halfback for Joe Simpkins Ford. Pariani and Peewee Wallace were in front of him on the line; Frank Borghi was in goal. The key game, most years, was against the Kutis Funeral Home—Harry Keough's team, St. Louis's other big power.

"We're playing Kutis this one time, it's late in the game"—Frank Borghi is remembering—"and the ball's out in front of my goal. I jump up to get it, and WHANG! I bang heads with Amiel Munoz, and it's like the lights went out. . . .

"Well, maybe half a minute later, I'm lying there on the ground all woozy, still about half knocked out. And up comes Charley. And he leans down over me, and he gets right in my face. 'Get up, you bum!' he says to me. 'Get up, you big bum! You're not hurt!'

"Well, I swear, I heard his voice, and I just rose like God. 'Okay, Charley,' I said. 'Okay, I'm ready to play.'

"The guy could inspire you. He didn't believe in being hurt. He didn't believe in quitting, not him or nobody else. He was a tough son of a bitch, the toughest I ever knew."

Charley Columbo died at home, on Elizabeth Avenue, where he had lived his whole life, in May of 1986, of cancer that had spread like brushfire from his lungs. He was sixty-five years old, a pack-a-day smoker since twelve.

His wife, Eleanor—whom he'd brought back with him from a Coast Guard stint in Seattle as a twenty-four-year-old bride in 1946—was on the phone to Frank Borghi within an hour of his death. It was the sort of call Borghi gets too many of these days. But with this one, he says, it was more than just the loss.

"I remember going to his house and then going to the room where he was. He was under a blanket, from his toes to his head. And I pulled the blanket back, and I saw him, and I just thought, 'Holy Christ, I thought the guy was indestructible.' But there he was. It was like looking at a ghost, there was nothing left of him; the cancer had eaten him alive. . . .

"And I just kept thinking, all the rest of that day—'Even Charley,' I kept thinking. 'Even him.' "

7

1st HALF

25:15

With twenty minutes left to play in the half, for the first time in the game, a save by Bert Williams halted play.

It came off a shot by Gino Pariani, from twenty yards out—a hurried, angled kick aimed high and to Williams's left. He stopped the ball easily—it was a less than perfect shot—catching it chest-high to stop play.

In the stands, for the first instant, there was silence. Then a sound. A single roaring sound, like a giant monster releasing its breath.

It had been nothing much to witness. A goalkeeper's workaday save. Yet to hear that roar from half a mile away, you'd have thought a war had been won. It shook the stadium—30,000 wordless voices, an indivisible, ejaculated bellow of sudden, hopeful shock.

Joe Gaetjens was on the ground when it happened, a yard or two in front of the English goal. He jumped to his feet, raised both arms overhead, and beat the air with his fist. The roar doubled. The crowd had been won.

．　．　．

It unsettled the English. They retook possession instantly, just short of midfield, off Bert Williams's clearing kick—then seemed suddenly, oddly throttled. They passed in the same tight patterns, but more tentatively now than before: Billy Wright to Laurie Hughes, Hughes back to Wright, back to Hughes, still short of midfield—as though awaiting reinforcements, or providence, or the dawning of a plan. No one in the crowd missed the difference. The stadium low-hummed.

Charley Columbo, at one point, lost patience. He charged Wright at midfield—recklessly, frontally, a near-hopeless assault. But Wright stumbled—on his own feet, it seemed—and the ball shot up vertically as though squeezed from a tube.

The hums turned to bellows. Every lung in the stands emptied air.

The English, again, retook possession. But their play was as rudderless as before. Their passes, still crisp, were now too often errant; they controlled the ball without effort, then surrendered it without cause.

They seemed almost hypnotized—their skills intact, their mastery still apparent. But now it was a mastery that lacked flow. Like a confused prizefighter, jabbing elegantly at a mirage.

Soccer is a game of tide shifts. They happen in a hundred ways. An unmarked winger, on a fullback's sideline pass, breaks suddenly free downfield. A back-shuffling midfielder, hoping only to break up play, improbably intercepts. A clearing kick is thwarted when a defender is stripped in the penalty zone—and possession changes, the dominance shifts.

Other reverses are grander, more sublime. A restive crowd, suddenly stirred, screams its blessings, waves its flags—and a dead-flat team summons wings. A shamelessly fouled teammate is carried from the field clutching his groin; his compatriots, suddenly empowered, take up his cause in a blitzkrieg of the rival goal. . . .

The rhythms of most sports rely on stop-and-start devisements:

four downs, nine innings, eighteen holes—and play is halted, breaths are caught, adrenaline depletes. In soccer, where play is continuous—there are no huddles, inning changes, set pieces, or lulls between tackles or points—the rhythms determine themselves. Twenty movable players in shifting patterns and constant flux, advancing and retreating in cadences that seldom repeat. Penalties are infrequent, substitutions few (until 1970, there were none allowed at all); when a man is injured, he is often not replaced.

Players, especially midfielders, run almost ceaselessly—five to ten miles a game, in five- to fifty-yard bursts—with no breathers for those winded, no shifts between units when the ball changes sides. Violence is intrinsic; emotions flow unchecked. It is the most fluid, elemental team sport in the world.

It has been played, in some form, since the beginning of recorded time. Ancient warriors played it with the heads of their victims; in the Aztec version, the losers lost their heads. In fifteenth-century Europe, whole villages played the game—one against the other, over miles of terrain, with few rules, frequent killings, and a hundred or more to a side.

It is less violent today, though nearly as simple. Seventeen rules govern it; the rulebook for U.S. football is as thick as your fist. Only the most basic statistics are kept: goals scored by minute, paid attendance, names of players and referee. Equipment is worn, not carried (no fiberglass, plastic, graphite, or wood). The only weapons are head and feet. And, except for the goalkeeper, there are no specialists on the field. All good fullbacks master dribbling; all forwards sometimes defend.

Simplicity makes for innovation. Because play is rarely stopped, players cannot anticipate defenses or script their routes in advance. They can only improvise. Because no one but the goalie is allowed to use his hands (a refinement of the English, the inventors of the modern game), creativity is spawned—head balls, chest traps, bicycle kicks, the feints and flourishes every skilled player makes his own.

In the absence of handheld weapons, goals are few and ever so precious. One (or even none, in the event of a scoreless tie, then settled by a shoot-out) can be enough to win a game. A well-struck goal, in a tight match between close rivals, is a crescendo without equal in sport.

"Soccer is such a difficult game"—George Vecsey would write, in the *New York Times*, more than thirty years after the game in Brazil—"its goals so precious, its fans so proprietary and passionate, that anybody who propels the ball into the net becomes a conquering hero, taking an ecstatic tour of the field, throwing kisses, leaping into the air, then falling to his knees as if in some ancient tribal ceremony."

With fifteen minutes left in the half, Wilf Mannion went down from a kick to the thigh. It wasn't serious—he was back on his feet within two minutes, and play was resumed—but in the space of time between whistles, the ten standing English players gathered in a knot near their goal.

It isn't known what was said in that huddle, or who did the talking or what was resolved, but the change could be seen from the stands. The ten disbanded silently, almost grimly, like a jury returning to court.

Play resumed seconds later. Jimmy Dickensen threw in to Mannion, mid-deep in the English zone. Mannion retreated briefly, a step or two, before turning and facing upfield. There were no retreats after that.

He punched ahead to Billy Wright at wing-half. Wright dueled briefly with Eddie Sousa, shook him off like a bug, then passed ahead to Stanley Mortensen, who was open on the left, just short of midfield. Mortensen carried forward several strides unchallenged, then was charged by Joe Gaetjens from his right.

He seemed for an instant not to see him—then stopped abruptly, pivoted, and turned sharply toward the center of the field. Gaetjens flew past, tottering like a dying top.

Mortensen was a playmaker, the finest on the English team. He dribbled now laterally, left to right, slowing as he went, more or less along the midfield line. The field shifted with him, behind and ahead—nineteen players spilling ballward, as bilgewater follows the listing of a ship. The left midfield emptied. The center was a blue-and-white knot.

The Americans marked closely, just across the midfield line. The English forwards were drawn in—a semicircular phalanx, a cross-weave of players thirty yards from end to end, five to eight yards in advance of the ball.

A yard past the center circle, Mortensen stopped, and turned, and seemed about to start upfield.

The field lurched. Mortensen kicked: a blistering, fast-rising, diagonal pass, upfield, left to right, thirty-five yards from point to point. The ball arced over the heads of the knotted players like a badly aimed missile, sliced the U.S. left-midfield as neatly as a pie square, then found the feet of Roy Bentley, full-sprinting down the right sideline, who'd broken free from the rear of the knot. Bentley trapped the ball now, uncontested, barely a yard inbounds, thirty yards to the right of the U.S. goal.

No ball exchange on any field of sport, no matter how practiced, could have been more flawless. There were cheers—awed, spontaneous, reluctant. Then silence.

The field thus carved, the English reset. There would be no further heroics. The passes now were tight, close-patterned, right-to-left:

Bentley in to Tom Finney; Finney back to Bentley, who crosses left to retake the striker's spot; Bentley over to Mortensen, another yard farther left—and the ball now is just right of center, twenty-three yards out, five yards outside the U.S. penalty zone.

But the Americans are pulled tight, crowding. Columbo is climbing Bentley's back; Harry Keough is a wall in front of Mortensen. There is no real hope of a shot. . . .

Mortensen back-heels to Billy Wright, who is just off his left shoulder, two yards behind—then breaks, in the same motion, for the goal. Keough, jump-started and outrun, has no chance at all. Seven English players now fan the U.S. goal. . . .

Wright is jammed, on his kicking side, by Walter Bahr. His shot is hurried but perfect: a short, lobbing pass that arcs just over the head of Charley Columbo, bisects the penalty line, and finds Mortensen alone—a step ahead of Keough, a yard to the right of the penalty mark, exactly twelve yards out from goal. There is only Frank Borghi to beat.

Borghi crouches, shortstop style, elbows just off knees, hands dangling, with four yards of open net on either side. It is a broadside shot, a 90 percent sure goal.

But Mortensen is too far under it. The ball sails. Rising a foot for every yard it travels, it clears the left-side crossbar by as much as four feet. A ridiculous, almost impossibly horrible shot.

Borghi has not moved a finger. Mortensen slams his fist into the upright as he carries past goal. The crowd is too stupefied to react.

This might have turned things, but it didn't. It was too late now for mood reversals. The English went back to work.

They passed, as before, in close patterns, shrinking the field in three-yard bites. Their domination remained total—almost embarrassing to watch. For the next eight minutes, the ball only twice, and only briefly, left the U.S. side of the field.

It was textbook English soccer. Tight, disciplined, patient, glacial. Pockets of the crowd booed. The majority were quiet, respecting the inexorable.

But there was something else, too, going on. For most of those minutes—for much of the game—as Tom Finney would say later to the press: "There was a gremlin in the U.S. goal."

It seemed true. In the thirty-first minute, Stanley Mortensen missed again. Just as strangely, another overkick from point-blank range, with Borghi as helpless as a trussed pig. A minute later, it was Finney himself, this time off a corner kick, headed perfectly, unstoppably, into the top-right corner.

Borghi guessed—it had to have been a guess; it couldn't have been anything more—and dove diagonally half the length of the goal, felt the ball slap off his right hand, then watched it sail, like a wing-shot pheasant, harmlessly over the bar.

And there were others. Borghi was uncanny—"El Magnifico," they would call him later. The English were off-target, the grass was too high, the field was too narrow, the goalposts were as wide as pillars. Blind luck was an animate force.

The Americans stayed game. They didn't panic. They felt the dominance and tried—and seemed—to adjust. They marked more closely. Their charges grew more considered, less headlong. The field, from the standpoint of both teams, became a succession of bunkers and grids.

But they were out of their depth here and must surely have known it. Parry-feint-parry was not the U.S. game. They could play it, if forced to, for a minute, or two, or five; just as a curveball pitcher, when the curve isn't breaking, can fall back on his fastball for a time. But it wasn't their strength. It wasn't what had gotten them here.

They were physical, straight-ahead players. They won with speed and strength and boldness, or not at all. Defensively, they were gamblers: charging, impetuous—"in your face" would be the term today. On the attack, their style was long, upfield passes that reached their targets more by muscle than art.

They were brawlers. In a pinch, defensive boxers. The English merely boxed.

It is forty-four summers later, in the waiting room of the Calcaterra Funeral Home, on Daggett Avenue, in the old neighborhood of Dago Hill. Frank Borghi, Gino Pariani, and Harry Keough are talking soccer: then versus now, the United States versus Europe, muscle versus art. And about how senseless, how downright priggish, the European style used to be.

Keough is telling one of his favorite stories, about Wilson T. Hobson, the coach of the 1948 U.S. Olympic team and an old-school sort of guy:

"So he says to his players before the game, 'Now, anytime your man gets away from you, what you gotta do is, you gotta yell "Check!" . . .'

" 'How come?' the players want to know. 'Well,' the coach tells 'em, 'because that's how they do it in field hockey, that's why.'

"Field hockey? Field hockey?"—Keough fairly shrieks now. "What the goddamn fuck's field hockey got to do with *anything*?"

The other two men explode, and slap their knees, but their friend isn't quite done:

"So I guess that team against Italy"—[who were beaten 9–0]—"they must have been running around that field all game long,

43

squawking like a bunch of goddamn chickens, just yelling out, 'CHECK' . . . 'CHECK' . . . 'CHECK.' "

In the thirty-seventh minute—the game still scoreless, still one-sided, the United States still miming the Englishmen's game—the ball went out of bounds off the foot of Tom Finney.

Walter Bahr took the throw-in from Eddie McIlenny, on the U.S. right side, ten yards inside the English zone. The English mid-fielders lay back. Bahr broke upfield—nearly twenty yards, unchallenged—before being charged by Billy Wright.

Bahr kicked—a shoulder-high, angled shot much like Pariani's of twelve minutes before, but from five yards farther out. The ball was well hit, but from too much distance to pose any threat. Bert Williams moved right for what looked to be his second save of the game.

"I took the shot from twenty-five yards out," Bahr remembers, "on the right-hand side of the goal. It was a decent kick—to the goalkeeper's right, to the opposite side. There was no question he had to make the move to the far post to get the ball. I'm sure he would have gotten the ball."

It is possible that no single instant of any soccer match has been more debated, or remains more a mystery, than the one that came next. Because what happened, as Harry Keough says today, "just couldn't have happened; it was just goddamn impossible."

The ball's path carried it diagonally over the penalty mark, twelve yards out from goal. As it passed over, Joe Gaetjens dove—twelve to fourteen feet is Keough's best guess—straight forward, straight out—"as though he thought he could fly or something; there's not another guy I know would have tried what he did."

He landed in a belly flop eight yards in front of the net. That much is known, was seen by 30,000 Brazilians and every man on the field. . . .

But somewhere along that fourteen-foot dive, some part of Gaetjens's head—the English press would say his right temple and call it an "accident," but nobody knows for sure—must have grazed some atom of the ball.

"It was like when we used to play softball, as kids," Keough says. "And you'd have this tree in center field. And a guy hits a fly ball, and you're under it to make the catch. . . . And it just grazes a leaf, and it changes path just that little bit—and it's just that same little bit, when you go to catch it, out of the pocket of your glove."

A picture survives in Frank Borghi's scrapbook. Badly faded now, taken from behind the English goal:

Bert Williams is in front of the right post, on his hands and knees on the ground, his body facing the sideline; an English defender stands over him, still looking toward the center of the field. Five yards behind Williams, and five yards to his left, is the ball—still in the air, a foot off the ground when the shutter is snapped, flush to the back of the net.

United States 1, England 0. Fifty-three minutes to play.

8

Harry Keough, at sixty-eight, has a memory you could only call awesome. There seems almost nothing he can't summon at will: grade-school seating orders, fifty-year-old addresses, the names of every teammate he ever played with, every score—and scorer—of every important game. When asked the order of things during the 1950 World Cup trip, he draws up a twenty-three-day calendar— June 17 to July 9—with notations in every box:

"Arr. San Juan 8:00 A.M.—12-hour delay, depart 10:00 P.M." . . . "to Rio via Trinidad & Belém, arr. 6:00 P.M. at City Hotel" . . . "Spain 3, USA 1" . . . "Practice in Rio" . . . "Killing time in Belém."

He also reads the morning paper without glasses, walks with his wife through Carondelet Park a mile and a half every day, coaches two soccer teams, has a quenchless thirst for Pepsi, and a full head of white hair. But it's the memory that stands out. He gets it from his father, he says.

Paddy Keough was night superintendent at the Laclede Gas Company in St. Louis. He had never gone to high school, but sat up

46

nights studying *Ridpath's History of the World* (he'd inherited it from his uncle), read the paper front-to-back every morning, and "was pretty much up on history, Napoleon, the classics, and all those things the average guy, you wouldn't think, would know a lot about. . . .

"I don't mean to say he was an intellectual or any of that. But my father, for a man of no real learning, he knew a lot of things.

"And he had common sense. His strong point—absolutely—his strong point was common sense. You want to hear my favorite? One of his gems, he used to say it all the time. . . .

" 'Ninety-eight percent of the time,' he'd say, 'ninety-eight percent of the time you can let your kids go their own way, let 'em do what they want. 'Cause if you've taught 'em even half right, they're going to pick the right thing. The other two percent, you gotta tell 'em no—tell 'em no and make it stick.'

"I've always remembered that. Practiced it with my own kids when the time came round. And you know what? It damn near always worked."

But more than anything else, Paddy Keough knew baseball. He knew baseball as well as any man alive.

"He liked the psychology of it. The mental part, I guess you'd say. He used to tell all these stories . . . about Ty Cobb, and how he'd sharpen his spikes, real slow, in front of everybody, right before the start of the game, just to get that other second baseman thinking, 'What's gonna happen when I take that first throw?'

"And about John McGraw [an early New York Giants manager], and how, when the teams would be trading sides during batting practice, he'd walk up to the guy who was gonna be pitching for the other team that day, and just kinda whisper in his ear, real soft: 'We're working on a trade, you might be with us next week. . . .'

"My dad, he loved those kind of stories. I'm not sure just where he got 'em all, but he got 'em somewhere; he was always reading up."

In 1955, Paddy Keough made it to the fifth round of *The $64,000 Question*—where they stumped him on the third part of a three-parter his son still swears was unfair. And he recalls, word for word, the question, all three answers ("seven answers, actually, if you count 'em one by one"), every aspect of the tale:

" 'In 1923, Babe Ruth batted .393, the highest average ever by a Yankee. One player has the highest average for three different teams. Name the player, the teams, and the averages.' . . .

"Well, it had to be Rogers Hornsby—that part was almost like a gift. And the first two teams were pretty easy—my dad got them both right away: the Cardinals in 1924, where he batted .424—nobody from St. Louis was going to miss that—and the Boston Braves in 1928, with an average of .387.

"But the third one was tough. He knew the team—the Chicago Cubs, 1930—and he knew the average was either .380 or .383; he couldn't remember which. . . .

"Well, figuring that when you're talking about Hornsby you go with the higher number, my dad chose .383. The right answer was .380.

"So it ended there. He didn't make the next round. They gave him a choice between $4,000 and a Cadillac. He took the $4,000 and came on home. . . .

"But hell, the question was a curveball to begin with; Hornsby's .380 didn't even lead the league that year. So how was anybody supposed to know?"

Harry Keough loved his father the way every father would want to be loved. He trusted him. He revered him. He made a lesson of his life. Even today, fourteen years after Paddy Keough's passing: "He was my idol as a person. I don't go a day of my life without quoting something he told me. He's just really inside my brain."

Everybody in town loved Paddy. He was the sort of man who made other men laugh and women feel special. He had a lifetime pass to Sportsmen's Park and went to every Cardinals home game until he was eighty-six—he died just short of ninety. He told baseball stories at weekly sports banquets, stood five-foot-five in his stocking feet but had "the widest smile in town." He played in old-timers games, year after year, until his legs wouldn't let him anymore.

"I remember watching him one time, digging out a triple—feeling proud, wondering if he was going to try to slide. . . ."

The eleven U.S. starters and coach in Belo Horizonte, June 29, 1950. *Bottom row, from left:* Frank ("Peewee") Wallace, Ed McIlenny, Gino Pariani, Joe Gaetjens, John ("Clarkie") Sousa, Eddie Sousa; *top row, from left:* Joe Maca, Charley Columbo, Frank Borghi, Harry Keough, Walter Bahr, Coach Bill Jeffrey. *(Courtesy National Soccer Hall of Fame)*

Borghi *(right)* and Bahr lead the U.S. team *(left)* onto the field in Mexico City, prior to their first World Cup qualifying match against Mexico *(at right)*, summer 1949. *(Courtesy National Soccer Hall of Fame)*

Columbo (4) and Keough (3) dispute a header with an English player at midfield. *(Courtesy National Soccer Hall of Fame)*

Stanley Mortensen *(dark jersey)*, Frank Borghi (1), and Charley Columbo (4) leap high to dispute an English cross. Walter Bahr *(at left, in the nearest white jersey)*, Gino Pariani *(in the background)*, and Ed McIlenny *(at right)* look on. *(Courtesy Frank Borghi)*

Fullback Harry Keough *(left)* races to clear the ball against England. Frank Borghi sets, ready for the worst. *(Courtesy National Soccer Hall of Fame)*

The ball has just left the foot of an English attacker, probably Finney *(far right)*. Borghi *(crouched, far left)* awaits it, with Walter Bahr *(left)* and Harry Keough by now out of play. *(Courtesy National Soccer Hall of Fame)*

Borghi saves one against England. *(Courtesy National Soccer Hall of Fame)*

1–0, USA: English goalkeeper Bert Williams, on his knees. The ball, already tipped by Joe Gaetjens, has passed to Williams's left and is behind him, flush to the net in back of the goal. *(Courtesy National Soccer Hall of Fame)*

Frank Borghi, minutes after the game, on the shoulders of Brazilian fans. *(Courtesy National Soccer Hall of Fame)*

Joe Gaetjens.
*(Courtesy National
Soccer Hall of Fame)*

Walter Bahr.
*(Courtesy National
Soccer Hall of Fame)*

Frank Borghi, goalkeeper for Simpkins Ford, around 1951. *(Courtesy Frank Borghi)*

The survivors. *Clockwise from top left:* Frank Borghi, Harry Keogh, Walter Bahr, John Sousa, and Gino Pariani at their final reunion in St. Louis, spring 1990. (*© Paul Harris*)

The author (*second row center*) with members of the Ravens and Harry Keough, at Pietro's Restaurant, St. Louis, October 1994. Frank Borghi is at the author's left, Keough to his right. (*Courtesy Frank Borghi*)

He told wild tales to his grandkids ("'Grandpa's sort of a hotdog, isn't he, Dad?' my daughter Colleen used to say"). He never drank. He never touched a child in anger ("he could do more just by looking at you"). He retired from the gas company at sixty-five—but went in every day for ten years after to run errands and pass out the mail.

Scores of public tributes marked his passing. The family favorite, a column by the *Globe-Democrat*'s Bob Burnes—"Little Paddy Keough Was a Big Man"—today hangs framed on Harry's sister's living-room wall.

"He was a fine man. That's what everybody always said, everywhere we'd go: 'Your father is a fine man.' When you hear that enough, from all of those people over all of those years, it kinda sticks with you. You feel proud. You want to be the same."

Of his mother, Elizabeth, who died seven years before her husband, he talks less; though when you hear what he does say (and how softly he says it), it's not hard to see why. He was a boy; she was a mother. Mothers didn't play baseball; they weren't heroes—they were only mothers—to their sons. The mechanics of family were simpler then.

"She never finished grade school. But she ran everything—without my Dad even knowing. She made things work. There wasn't much she didn't do."

He is reminded, as he says this, of a story he once heard from a priest at the fiftieth anniversary party of some old family friends. "I'm reminding myself of a lot of things now," he says. "A lot of things are coming back."

He chuckles, more in delight than amusement. "It's good to remember. It's good to go back. . . .

"The story was, There are these two old guys, see, and they get to talking. And the one guy, he says to the other, 'So, how did your marriage last so long?'

"And the second guy, he says, 'Well, all I know is that when we got married I said to my wife, 'Look,' I told her, 'the things that are not too important? That's your department; you handle those. I'll take care of the important stuff. Understood?'

" 'Yeah, okay,' she says, 'understood.'

" 'So how did it work out?' the first guy asks. 'Worked out great,' says the second guy. 'No really big things ever came up. . . .'

"That's about how it was with my folks. My mom just took care of stuff. My dad, I don't think he even knew."

He was forty-seven when his mother died. Over all of those years of knowing her, he can recall only a single piece of advice: " 'Get a steady job, Harry, something you can count on. And then hold on to it. . . .'

"Well, I worked thirty-five years for the U.S. Post Office. I guess that'd be steady enough to suit her. I guess she'd be happy with that."

The world needs more Harry Keoughs: untroubled, life embracing, age defying, the son of a "fine man" with a passion for baseball, of a mother who "made things work." Those sorts of things carry over. They stick with you; you remember them. And the cycle—like most cycles, bad or good—carries on.

"When I see things on TV sometimes—you know, divorce, wife beatings, the things they do to kids today—it makes me realize . . . I guess I used to think everybody had the steady, safe kind of life we had at home. I didn't know any different then.

"But now—I guess not too many people did. Or maybe they just don't anymore, I don't know. I never would have said we had a perfect family, but . . . " And the rest trails off, unsaid.

He began with the post office on the fourteenth of June, 1948. He was twenty years old, just home from the navy, still single. His starting pay was eighty cents an hour; his first year, including overtime, he made $2,870. "A lot of money in those days," he says. "My first house payment was $49.25 a month."

He carried the mail on foot—in thirty-pound shoulder bags, starting at six in the morning, over an eight-mile route of homes. He would do this eighteen years, until he made supervisor—$7,421 a year—in the spring of 1966, and his duties moved inside.

His mornings after that began earlier (at five A.M.), but his days were over by one. So he took a second job, as head coach of the

St. Louis University men's soccer team, which would win five national titles in the sixteen seasons he was there.

He would retire from the post office in the fall of 1982, on a pension of $17,000, almost six times his first year's pay. His home would be paid for—a thirty-year mortgage paid off in twenty-one. Two of three children would be married and gone. He would have just buried his father, just welcomed his first grandchild. He would be fifty-five years old.

But at twenty, as an eighty-cent-an-hour mailman trainee, he had only one real talent in life. And at that he was very, very good.

A former junior-team national champion, as a seventeen-year-old, with the Schumacker Undertakers; a standout in the mid-1940s with the Spanish Society junior team; a longtime regular in Dent McSkimming's "Soccer Shots" column of the *St. Louis Post-Dispatch*. A year later, in the summer of 1949, he would play for the U.S. national team.

Two months before his twenty-first birthday, in September of 1948, he started at halfback for Paul Schulte Motors—which, a season later, would become McMahon Pontiac, and a year after that, Zenthofer Furs. He would play for them three seasons (under all three sponsors' names), before leaving, in the fall of 1952, to play for the Kutis Funeral Home.

"In those days, there was three newspapers in town. And all three of them, you know, they covered soccer pretty good. And this one guy—an Austrian guy, his name was Nick Jost—he sponsored a team called the Raiders. He deserves a lot of credit; he figured out how to make that work. . . .

"He had this scrapbook he kept, that he took around town. And he'd go, and he'd sit down with some car dealer or undertaker or something, and he'd open up his scrapbook, and show the guy all the headlines and all—you know, 'Kutis Beats Simpkins,' 'McMahon versus D'Andreas,' that kinda thing. . . .

" 'That could be you,' he'd say to the guy. 'How would that be— the name of your company in the paper every week? Just like free advertising. All you gotta do is pay for some sneakers and balls. . . .'

"And the guy, a lotta times anyway, would sign up. . . ."

•   •   •

They played at Sportsmen's Park, the Northside Softball Stadium, and half a dozen municipal fields. The fields were rented by the sponsors; the soccer shoes, uniforms, shin guards, and balls were purchased and given free. And from time to time—depending on the sponsor, and the sort of year it was—there might be a little something more.

"Playing for Kutis, when Christmastime came, all the players knew what to expect: fifty bucks and a turkey to take home. Tom Kutis, he was a very generous man. . . .

"Other times, it was different things. Like for a while, the league had this system—you'd get six dollars for a win, four for a tie, two for a loss—and they'd put it all in a kitty and hold it for you till the season was through. Or maybe the owner would kick in twenty bucks for every goal you scored, or something like that. . . .

"The best year we ever had, at the end of the season there was close to two hundred dollars in the pot. Not a total of two hundred dollars, either; two hundred dollars for every guy on the team. That was big money. And what made it better, we got it all at once."

He had learned the game, as not much more than a toddler, from his older brother Bill—at about the same time that Gino Pariani, on a Dago Hill playground five miles northwest, was learning it from his older cousin Mike. Family teaching family. And in much the same way.

"It was 1932, '33—the middle of the Depression. I'm five or six years old; my brother's maybe fifteen. They're out there on the [Blow School] playground every day after school—twelve, thirteen, fourteen, maybe even twenty guys on a side; nobody had a job in those days—playing some pick-up game. And there I am, chasing balls behind the goal."

(As he recalls all this—"and they're out there . . . and there I am"—he smiles softly, a little goofily. His eyes fix themselves on a spot in the center of the living-room wall, behind which—it is not so hard to guess—a little Irish kid in baggy shorts speeds to close the gap on his big brother's soccer ball.)

"In the summer, the game changed. Fast-pitch softball. But it was pretty much the same deal. Bill and the guys would be playing; I'd be shagging foul balls. . . . But hey, he was my big brother, my number-one hero in life. I'd have done anything he asked me to."

Bill Keough would go on to play for the Chicago Manhattans, a semipro soccer team named for a beer brand now long since defunct, then to gain small fame as "Willy Keo" of the "Willy Keo and His Dry-Diving Act" trampoline comedy show. For more than thirty years—until a broken leg forced him to quit at sixty-four—at state fairs and police circuses throughout the Midwest, he would do double somersaults off three-meter boards (" 'double or triple,' he always used to say, 'the average guy don't know the difference, but everybody can laugh' "), mock-drunk or dressed in clown suits—landing, always barely, often on his duff, on a small circle of rubber and rope.

The Evel Knievel of the carny circuit. He made a living at it, though his mother, Elizabeth, could not have been pleased. He is seventy-eight today, still a hero to his brother the postman, who brags about his feats without end.

Harry Keough's house today is a lot like he is. Warm, easy, unstylish. A mantelpiece cuckoo chirps on the hour; the chairs are made for sitting, the kitchen is spotless, the carpeting thick. He is at the dining-room table, in a cubicle off the kitchen you could only call a "dinette," in a blue sweatsuit and bright white sneakers, talking easily, sipping—always—from a Pepsi. ("Harry likes his sody," says his old friend Frank Borghi. "When Harry comes over, you got to have plenty of sody around.")

Alma Keough, his bride of forty-three years, comes and goes from the room, offering small comments ("all this talk about his memory, but he can't remember what he ate for lunch"), clearing off dishes, replenishing coffee and Pepsi. But mostly she stays apart.

"When Harry gets talking about soccer," she says, "there's nothing to do but listen. And I heard all the stories before."

Her husband smiles dutifully; she pats his shoulder on her way back past his chair. Outside, along a street of tidy, 1950s-era ranch houses, a dozen sprinklers bob and hiss through a mid-June afternoon.

"I grew up a mile west of here," he says. "I've never lived out of St. Louis except to go in the navy." Proud statements both.

They lived on Vermont Avenue, in the Spanish section of town: Paddy, Elizabeth, their two daughters and two sons—Harry is the youngest of four—a lone Irish family in an enclave of Cantabrian Spain.

(Most other St. Louis Irish lived at the time in what remained of two once-proud neighborhoods, Tipperary and Kerry Patch—both by then in the last stages of a decades-long death.

"About my block, of which I was so proud, there were no foreigners in it," a local Irishman, Jack Ryan, recorded later. "The neighbors were the McClanns, the O'Reillys, the Haggartys, the O'Briens. . . . Johnny Corrigan's block? It became ruined. A family named Schweitzer moved in.")

The Keoughs' neighborhood was poor—the sons and daughters of zinc miners from the province of Asturias, who worked slavish hours for low pay in the city's foundries and plants. The work was not steady; unemployment on Vermont Avenue was among the highest in town. No one had a dollar that didn't go for bread or rent.

"The YMCA, near where we lived, it cost three dollars a year to belong. To use the pool, you paid five cents a month. Most of the Spanish couldn't afford it, except they let this one club, the Caballeros, swim once a week for free. . . .

"But they didn't let the Spaniards into the gym too much. I'll tell you why. They'd get in there, they'd start kicking the basketballs and volleyballs around, start playing soccer with 'em, you know, breaking the lights and the windows and all that.

"The guys who ran the place, it used to drive 'em nuts—'Keep that Harry Keough and the rest of them spics outta the gym!' this one guy used to say.

"I got a real kick outta that, him thinking I was Spanish. Except you can't really tell, I guess, by just hearing my name. You gotta see it spelled."

They played soccer wherever there was space. On the field behind the Susan Blow School; on a riverfront tract they called "the Spanish lot"; in back of a foundry, with lots of white sand for the marking of lines. And later, as teenagers, at Carondelet Park with the Schumacker Undertakers junior team.

"My first year with Schumacker was the fall of forty-three. It was mostly Spanish, some Italians—Frank and Gino, they were both on that team. Only one other Irish kid, his name was O'Toole."

He speaks lovingly of those times. The neighborhood, the soccer, the hardscrabble life of his teammates and friends. "If we'd lived anywhere else but where we did," he says, "I'd probably never have learned the game."

But it goes deeper than that—deeper than soccer—and he knows it. Harry Keough, for all the Irishness of his fair, jowly, deep-dimpled face, is an Irishman only by blood. His heart, his loyalties, the choices he has made, are as Spanish as the block of Vermont Avenue he still sometimes, in unwitting moments, calls "home."

Other boys on other blocks talked of Musial and DiMaggio, the brilliant (and hated) Yankees, the Cardinals' pennant hopes. Around Vermont Avenue supper tables, the names were different: Zamora, Langara, Barcelona, Real Madrid. Or—in older company, in other moods—Franco, the Asturias miners' revolt, the fascist Falange, the Spanish Civil War.

Over time, by slow osmosis, he adopted much of it. The heroes, the stories, the hand-me-down heritage of a migrant people's trials. ("They came from Asturias, in the north," he says thoughtfully, and spells the name of the province, then rolls it twice off his tongue, mouthing every syllable as though teaching a small child to talk. "They settled in colonies—Terre Haute, St. Louis, pockets of Kansas, Denora, Pennsylvania, those were the main ones, I think. . . . In small cities mostly, where there were mines or foundries, the sorts of jobs they knew. They were poor, and not educated, but they weren't afraid of hard work. . . .")

What didn't come by osmosis, he brought about by will. "I wanted to learn the language. I'd grown up hearing it, I knew some words and phrases and all; but I couldn't put them together, I couldn't speak with the guys."

He went to the Spanish Society—"kind of a community center, I guess you'd call it, with a big hall upstairs, where the old guys went to play cards." He borrowed some books, studied the Spanish newspapers. When he thought he was ready, he began practicing on everyone in sight.

"And inside of a year, maybe less, I was doing pretty good." He has been fluent ever since.

One of those he practiced on was a seventeen-year-old Mexican named Ruben Mendoza, a teammate for two seasons with McMahon Pontiac/Zenthofer Furs.

"Kind of a small kid, and young. But real skilled for his age—for any age. A heck of a player. Three years later, he made the national team."

One of Mendoza's biggest fans was a fifty-year-old family friend—and fellow Mexican—named Salvador Flores, a regular at the Mc-Mahon/Zenthofer games. He and Harry got to know each other.

"I spoke Spanish with him. I think he sort of liked that. We got to be pretty good friends."

In the early spring of 1951, a Mexican guitar trio, "the Norteños," were playing at a local hotel-bar—"Perfidia," "Cielieto Lindo," "La Paloma." (He translates: " 'Perfidious,' that means treacherous, that means she was cheating on him. . . . Beautiful songs, love songs, most of 'em—you ought to hear 'em some time. . . .")

Flores approached the group. His wife, he told them, was coming up on a birthday. Would they play at a party at his home?

"He invited me. I went along. And that was the night I met Alma—April the second, 1951. And the rest, I always say, is Ruben Mendoza's fault."

He laughs. It is one of his old standards. He has a million of them.

Alma Flores, Salvador Flores's oldest daughter, was twenty-one years old. Although born in St. Louis, she had left when she was two, to return with her parents to Guadalajara after her father had lost his railroad job. When the job reopened some years later, her father and mother came back. But Alma stayed on, living with a succession of cousins and aunts.

"Her life was in Mexico," says her husband today. "She'd never really known it here. She didn't like the climate anyhow."

She was at her parents' home that April only to visit—perhaps (she can't recall) for her mother's birthday. She planned to stay two weeks.

She spoke no English. He offered to teach her; she had no real wish to learn. They went to the movies ("I translated; she watched; the people around us moved away").

She extended her visit. He'd known her two months when he proposed ("in Spanish; I wanted to be sure she understood"). They were married in August of 1952.

She is sixty-six today. Pretty, petite, young looking, still with the easiness of a girl. She laughs almost constantly—it's hard to imagine her without at least a smile—and jokes with every other breath.

"Harry, he taught me his English. And that is why I speak so good."

She mouths each word singly, exaggerating her accent, no doubt intending the mangled adverb. They both laugh. You can tell it's another old joke.

Their fondness for each other is so instinctive and familiar, so interwoven with the patter they share, it is easy to mistake for jest.

He has been telling a story about a high-school girlfriend named Lois ("I kinda took her for granted; I didn't treat her so good"), who'd written him finally, on a destroyer in the Pacific midway through his navy tour, to tell him that she'd met another boy.

"My good friend Andy Gonzalez—from the old neighborhood, we go back a long way—he asked me maybe six years after that, 'Harry,' he says, 'you ever think about Lois? You ever wonder how things might have been?'

"And I told him.—'Andy,' I said, 'for the longest time, I always used to think that no matter who I married, no matter how things ended up, I'd always think to myself, "Harry, you dumb son of a bitch, you never had it better; Lois was the only one for you."

" 'But you know what?'—and this is just how I said it to him—'I got this woman now, Andy, she's just so perfect, so much more for me. I feel like sometimes there was never anybody else. . . .'

"I saw Lois maybe ten years ago, at our class reunion. Now, I don't mean to say she looked bad, but not so good either—not near as pretty as Alma. And Alma, she knew it, too, and she sorta like laughed—not in front of Lois, of course. . . .

"And I said, 'Well, I guess I know how you feel; I was kinda relieved myself when I saw that old boyfriend of yours in Mexico that time, and what he looked like.' "

Alma has not been present during this. She arrives now, home from some errand, her arms full of boxes and bags.

"I was just talking about Lois," he begins—but it isn't the story that interests him now. He chops it short, cutting quickly to the punch line: "not near as pretty as Alma."

He smiles, a little slyly. His wife laughs, then protests: "Oh Harry, Harry, don't tell me these are the stories you been telling this man . . ." But the laugh is more of a giggle, and it's easy to see she is pleased.

All three children are grown now, all married, each with children of their own. Their son, Ty, is a college soccer coach. Colleen works at a local law school; Peggy is part owner of a travel agency in town. All three families live within a fifteen-minute drive.

Harry and Alma go away together often. Usually to Mexico, where Alma's family still lives. Her father, Salvador, is ninety-four today ("not doing so good, just kind of hanging on"). Her mother, Maria Luisa, whose birthday made their union forty-five years ago, died in her sleep in 1991.

They still see Ruben Mendoza, who turned sixty-four last year. Harry's toast to him at his birthday was just what you'd expect: "And the rest is Ruben Mendoza's fault. . . ."

He laughs as he tells this. Everybody laughs. Their lives seem made of laughter.

Outside of Alma, his first love remains soccer. He is head coach for the Block Yeshiva High School, assistant coach of the Washington University women's team (his son, Ty, is coach of the men's)—and honorary "handshaker" at as many U.S. team games as he wants to make it to.

("In my opinion, and I'm not just bragging"—says Frank Borghi, who brags endlessly about everybody but himself—"this is the man, right here, who should be coaching the U.S. national team. . . .")

Until four years ago, he played halfback every Sunday in the local fifty-five-and-over league. He was sixty-four when he quit. ("My knees, they wouldn't do the job no more.") At least once a year, he makes the trip to Oneonta, New York, to accept some new honor at the U.S. Soccer Hall of Fame.

His wife's life is more homebound, but no less busy.

" 'What do I do?' " Alma Keough asks now, repeating the question. "How you mean, 'What do I do?' I am—how they say it?—I am a housewife. I clean, I cook. Some days I watch the soaps. Mexican, not American. In the American soaps, the story, it go on thirty years; you could die before it ends. . . ."

But mostly, she cooks. "I cook all day some days, half the week long. All week long. All week long, I cook for Sunday. . . ."

She laughs. She has heard herself; sometimes, when she hears herself, it makes her laugh out loud. Sundays, she says, are "for the family." They are her favorite days. Still, there's a lot of cooking involved.

"Ty, Colleen, Peggy—and the wives or husbands, they all got wives or husbands now. And the grandkids—five girls, can you believe that? Five girls we got, and still they got no boys? I think it's time for a boy. . . . And Harry's sister number one, and Harry's sister number two—they live next door, you know—and Harry's brother Bill. . . .

"They all come. And others too, sometime. They watch TV—baseball, soccer—they eat all different things. So Sunday dinner is for the family. I cook sometime all week."

Sixteen for Sunday dinners. Three generations—the oldest seventy-eight, the youngest not yet two—filling the rooms and corners, Sunday after Sunday, of the little house at 7325 Rainor Court.

And Grandpa's still a "hotdog." And Grandma "makes things work." And with each new fiancé or in-law, the question that stumped Paddy Keough gets retold.

"It's good," he says, "to keep that stuff alive. It's okay to move forward, but once in a while you gotta look back."

9

T he ball was still in the back of the English net, the crowd roar had only just peaked, when Harry Keough turned to Joe Maca at midfield.

"Holy Christ," I told him, "I think we just woke 'em up. Hold on to your hat, Joe. All hell's gonna break loose now."

It had happened so fast. And so absurdly. A flying leap, a fluke head-graze, a blind-luck goal not a man on the field had even seen. Only Joe Gaetjens, Harry Keough would say later—"Only Joe would have tried something as crazy as that. . . . And even Joe, if he was alive and sitting here now, I'll bet he couldn't tell you how that ball made it in."

For a full half minute, the roar was deafening. The air itself seemed to vibrate. The old wooden stands swayed like tent-posts in a gale.

It was the loudest roar ever heard in Belo Horizonte. Small children joined in it, then stopped, suddenly frightened, and trembled in their fathers' chests. The Italian referee, on his way to the center circle to put the ball back in play, plugged his ears against the noise.

60

They heard it in the diamond mines in the hills above the city; on the farms around it; and in the city itself, through shut windows and closed doors. From a distance, some would say later, it did not seem a human roar.

It lasted—thunderous, unrelenting—until the instant Roy Bentley touched the ball to restart play. Then, with every second that followed, it seemed to die a bit—imperceptibly, a decibel or two— until, by a minute or so after play had resumed, there was barely a sound from the stands.

Perhaps they were simply roared out. Or feared, as Harry Keough did, that the English lion, now wounded, would rise from its torpor and the butchery would begin. Or perhaps they were only confused.

They had to have been confused. They'd been screaming their lungs out for a band of 500–1 ragamuffins who wore cowboy hats and boxing mittens and played soccer as though they'd learned it in a bar. The closest thing to a "victory" any of them could have dreamed of was a 4–0 or 5–0 English win—"Brits Struggle against Hapless Americans," the next day's headlines would read, and thirty million Brazilians would feed on the hope.

That would have been more than good enough to send them home happy, more than worth their afternoon's time.

But here it was, nearly half the game gone, and the ragamuffins were leading. What were they to think now?

Friday's headlines ("Brits After 37 Minutes: Scoreless, Stymied, Staring at Defeat") were probably already assured—no matter what might come next. Should they not be content with that? Or should they pin their hopes to a vision and scream themselves hoarse till it burst?

They grew quieter by the second, even as the Americans hung on doglike, and the clock ran down on the half.

The English didn't lose their poise. But neither did "hell break loose," as Harry Keough had foretold.

They controlled play, as before. They were as precise, as economical—and as dominant—as at any time in the game. For the final eight minutes of the first half of play, they held possession for close to seven. They took two more clean shots—the first by Mortensen, the second by Finney—for a total of fourteen in the half.

The Americans took none, came close to none (for a total of two). Frank Borghi remained brilliant. The fullbacks remained staunch. In all things, they were much as before: a band of mailmen and sheet stackers, saved from comedy only by their grit.

The whistle blew with the ball on Tom Finney's foot, fifteen yards out from the U.S. goal.

Finney shot—an unstoppable shot, a foot inside the left post, eighteen inches off the ground. But Frank Borghi, by the time the ball hit the net behind him, was already walking away.

The crowd cheered; "lustily" would probably best describe it. But it was a cheer now, no longer the roar of before. About half the 30,000 stood in tribute. One young boy in the third or fourth row, atop his father's shoulders, waved a small American flag.

United States 1, England 0. Forty-five minutes to play.

10

HALFTIME

As far as anyone can remember, there wasn't much said in the locker room between halves.

Gaetjens and Borghi got their fair share of backslaps; there were some queries from the defense as to how the goal had been scored. ("It was Walter there that kicked it," Gaetjens told them. "All I did was dive.") But no pep talk or strategy session. Coach Jeffrey, as nearly as Harry Keough recalls it, didn't have ten words to say.

" 'Well played, lads, keep it up'—he might have said something like that. But nothing much worth remembering. What was he going to say? He wasn't going to make any changes; we were a goal up on those guys. And he couldn't get all positive sounding—he had to figure it'd never hold up."

There wasn't a player among them who thought it would hold up. Not one, not even remotely. They knew the history. Half of them had been part of it: 0–9 against Italy, 0–5 against Northern Ireland, 0–11 against Norway, 0–4 against Scotland—most in the past twenty months. And that didn't include Mexico—twice—the previous summer, or the Istanbul Besitkas, or the English club team in New York. Or Spain in Curitiba, only four days before.

They were bad. Horrible—by the standards of anywhere but the United States. Whipping boys to the humblest teams in the world. And they knew it. It was a running joke. ("If you can't cry about something," says Keough, "well then, you may as well laugh.")

They made bets on the tallies against them, joked with reporters about bringing cribbage boards to keep score. They called Frank Borghi the "six-goal wonder"—he'd once allowed six goals several games in a row. "I gotta hand it to you, Frank," Peewee Wallace had said to him then, "you really got their number now."

They were always joking about something. It kept them loose. It kept their pride intact. They joked, and made bets and wore crazy outfits, played the best soccer they knew how, and defined victory in relative terms. And even by these standards (anything within four or five goals, against the best teams, was considered to be a good day), they almost never won.

So to be ahead of England by a goal at halftime, to have held Spain to a 3–1 score—they were a jolly group in the locker room that day. And whatever talking might have been done, it probably wasn't serious. It probably wasn't even about the game.

Bahr and Keough may have been the brains of the team. Columbo was the gutsiest. Frank Borghi probably had the biggest heart. But laughter was what kept them going. And it was Peewee Wallace, hands down, who led them in that.

He was, to begin with, a funny-looking man. As skinny as a pencil, with arms too long for his body, and shoulders that seemed barely wide enough to support his neck. His hair was dark and receded, and rolled in a succession of valleys and foothills across the top of his head. His nose was half the length of his face. He looked like a scarecrow with a pompadour.

Perhaps, as a boy, it had been his looks that shaped his first view of things—taught him laughter as medicine, kept him away from the self-seriousness of other young girls and boys. Perhaps it was then, as a five-year-old, as a means of survival, that he'd first become a clown.

However it happened, he was a natural. Effortless, deadpan (or mock serious), with an instinctive sense of the comic or absurd—one of those people who can find humor in a corpse.

No one who knew him can recall him any other way. It was as though he'd seen life as comedy by the time he'd hit second grade:

> "Frankie Wallace, get back to your seat right now."
>
> "But Miss Smithers, the gerbil is peeing. It's peeing straight up in the air."
>
> "The gerbil is doing its business, Frankie. That has nothing to do with this class."
>
> "But it does, Miss Smithers, it does. . . . You told us once that upside-down could mean rightside-up, that it depends on where you're looking from—that if the person who was looking was standing on his head . . . But I'm not. . . .
>
> "But the gerbil, I think, he's standing on his head. And he's peeing straight up in the air. So I was just wondering . . ."

Even his name—Wallace—was a joke. The real one, the Italian one, was Valecenti. It had been changed—"Americanized"—by some ancestor, two or three generations before, but had remained on the rolls at Immigration, where he discovered it when he went for his passport in the spring of 1950, just prior to the trip to Brazil. He never adopted it; he remained Wallace to the last. But he had fun for a while with the "twin brother" jokes.

"He was probably the funniest man I ever knew," Harry Keough says today. "And he never even tried. He'd say something—as straight-faced as you please—and everybody else, they'd start laughing their guts out. And Peewee, he'd just sort of stand there looking at you, like he didn't have a clue what all the fuss was about."

The two of them—Wallace and Keough—were in Mexico City in the summer of 1949, midway through the regional tryouts, which would land them in Brazil the next year:

"We were walking down the street there one day, and there's this truck going by, with this sign on the side: 'Esquela de Peros'—that's Spanish for 'Dog School.'

"Well, I'd never heard of that before. So I said to somebody,

'What's that mean, "Dog School"? Is that a dog catcher or something?' No, they said, that was an ad for rich people—to get them to
train their dogs to do things and all. So we took that in. . . .

"Then maybe two, three days later, Peewee and I, we're walking
along again—and he's got that big cigar in his mouth, you know.
It's the end of the day; the sun's behind us, just about to go down.
And along comes this little old dog. His coat's all mussed up, there's
mud matted all over him, eyes all sad and all—a real wreck of a
dog.

"Well, Peewee, he don't miss a beat. He takes one look at him,
pulls that cigar out of his mouth, looks him straight in the eye, like
the dog was human or something.

" 'Hey *you*,' he says, 'hey you—I'm talkin' to *you* there! How
come you're not in school?' "

Frank Borghi has been listening through all this, smiling and nod-
ding, though he has heard the story a dozen times at least. The
punch line comes—"How come you're not in school?"—and he
roars, a thunderous, room-filling roar. Then recovers, and begins
shaking his head slowly from side to side. He looks, for several seconds, sad enough to cry.

"Funniest guy I ever knew," he says. "Just a beautiful guy. . . .
Hey, Harry, now we're on dog stories—you ever hear the one about
Harry Desmond?"

Keough has, of course. But the question is only a courtesy. He
smiles slightly, and Borghi is off.

"We're playing this game one day, at Sportsmen's Park" [Wallace
and Borghi, together with Gino Pariani and Charley Columbo, were
teammates with Joe Simpkins Ford], "and it's between halves, you
know, and Frank and I, we're climbing the steps back up to the
clubhouse. . . .

"And there was this halfback playing for us then. Harry Desmond.
A great big guy, probably six-foot-four, and real strong, but not one
of the better halfbacks around. And Desmond, even for him, it's
been a bad day.

"So we're climbing the steps, just talkin' and all. And there's this
big old dog, laying there on the top steps, not paying us no attention,
just laying out there on the steps.

"And Frank, all of a sudden he stops, and he just looks at the dog.

" 'You,' he says, and he points his finger in the dog's face. 'You. You're in for Desmond in the second half.' "

Frank Wallace was eleven years old, and Frank Borghi had just turned nine, when the two first met—as softball opponents in the spring of 1934, on a playground field on Dago Hill. Wallace was a Wildcat, Borghi a Raven. ("We had about thirty, forty teams on the Hill in those days: the Ravens, the Stags, the Wildcats, the Gloom Chasers, the Hawks. I can't remember half the names anymore. . . .")

As teenagers, they were teammates with the Catholic Youth Club. ("Softball in the summer, soccer in the winter; we were together every day nine months of the year.") Then came the war. Borghi was shell-shocked in Normandy. Wallace, captured by the Germans at Anzio, spent sixteen months in a POW camp.

"Were you ever in the service?" Keough remembers a reporter asking him once. " 'Yeah,' says Peewee, 'I was in the service.' And that's all he ever said about that."

They returned, the war over, and were teammates again: for ten years and two national championships, with Simpkins Ford. ("Before every home game at Sportsmen's Park, in the locker room, I'd give him two cigars. Every game, two cigars. It was just this thing we did.")

Wallace, at least half of those years, was the team's star and high scorer. Borghi, by some accounts, was the finest goalkeeper in the United States. In his tattered old scrapbook of newsclips, it's hard to find a page that doesn't record the feats of both:

> For the fifteenth time since 1920, St. Louis has placed a team in the final round of the United States Open Soccer Championship. Winning from the Morgan club here yesterday, 2–0, on goals by Gino Pariani and Frank Wallace, the clever Joe Simpkins team won the right to represent the Western Division in the grand final. . . .
>
> A major share of the credit for scoring the shutout

> in the face of the home team's reckless charge goes
> to goaltender Frank Borghi. . . .

> Regarding the Simpkins chances of taking the na-
> tional title, it may be safely prophesied that the team
> will go just as far as Frank Wallace can take it. Wal-
> lace, the man who scored both goals in defeating
> Kutis in the Open Cup game, drove home the goal
> that broke a tie score, two minutes before the end of
> the first half. . . .

> Outstanding for the victors was goalie Frank Borghi.
> Had he not exercised uncanny judgement, combined
> with cat-like agility, in parrying a dozen fine Kutis
> shots, there would have been no opportunity for
> Frank Wallace to score the two points that won the
> game. . . .

> One minute before the end of the half, Frank Wal-
> lace put the Simpkins ahead 2–1 when he drove a
> bullet-like shot into the corner after taking a pass
> from Bertani. Wallace's shot was virtually unstop-
> pable. . . .

Neither man ever had a closer friend. One was best man at the
other's wedding; the other was godfather to the first man's third son.
They were roommates on road trips. When Wallace took up golfing,
Borghi—who, at the time, had never played golf in his life—tagged
along.

"I didn't know you were supposed to be quiet; I'd never played a
quiet sport before. So I'd be standing there behind him, talking
away. . . .

" 'Dammit, Frank,' he'd say to me, 'dammit'—and he'd give me
this look—'can't you see I'm trying to concentrate?' "

Borghi the ingenuous, for half a lifetime, played straight man to
Wallace the wit.

"We were somewhere on some road trip"—now it is Keough, the
memory-marvel, who recalls—"and Peewee, he looks over at Frank

and he says: 'So Frank, how're you gonna spend that seventy-five bucks [Coach] Numi gave us for meals?'

"And Peewee, you know, he kinda sneaks me this look. I can see what he's up to, so I keep my mouth shut. . . .

" 'Whaddaya mean, seventy-five dollars?' Frank says. 'I only got fifty.'

" 'Well, Frank, what can I tell you?' Peewee says then. 'Some guys are just more valuable than others.' "

"I guess if I was a gay person, they'd probably say we were lovers."

He laughs as he says this. But it is an awkward laugh. And for a moment or two, there is silence—until his wife's voice breaks it, disembodied, from a room away:

"He was your best friend, Frank. You *loved* the man. He was your best friend in the world."

"Yeah," he says then. "He was. He was my best friend. My roomie. He was like a brother to me. I carry his picture with me—I just liked that man so much."

Peewee Wallace wouldn't score that day against England—although once, in the game's final minutes, he would be robbed by Alf Ramsey of what many felt, even so, was a score. ("Wallace . . . outran fullback Aston to the penalty area," one news account would report later, "drew goaltender Williams far out, beat him with a feint, and crossed the ball toward the empty goal. Ramsey, the right fullback . . . arrived just in time to reach the ball as it was about to cross the line for a point. . . .") But three days later, against Chile, he headed in a corner kick in the second half to tie the game.

"He was one of those guys who could beat you a hundred ways," Keough remembers. "As a player, he was in a class by himself. Not big, not tough looking, but just so gifted, so versatile. . . . He could play any line position, kick off either foot, score from anywhere on the field. And aggressive. Nobody was more aggressive than Peewee. But I never saw him take a cheap shot. Never. He beat you clean, or he didn't beat you at all. . . .

"You hear this all the time today about athletes, so I guess you probably won't use it; but in the case of Peewee, it's the truest thing I could say. He was a classy guy, on the field and off. . . ."

.   .   .

In the spring of 1978, he was diagnosed with brain cancer. He was fifty-six years old. He died slowly, mostly painlessly, over the next eighteen months—the last several of them in a St. Louis hospice, where Frank Borghi's daughter Betty used to go on weekends to play him tunes on her guitar.

Just after the tumor had been found and the doctors had reclosed his head and told him his time would be short, Borghi himself went to see him.

"It was a Sunday morning when they called. I went right over. He was in intensive care, he had a skullcap covering his head and all, and I had to put this drape thing on me, this white drape. And I walked into his room, and he takes one look at me. . . .

" 'Don't you *touch* me!' he says. 'Don't you dare *touch* me!' "

"I'd never seen him like that. I didn't know what to say. 'Aw c'mon, Frank,' I said—I was trying to kid him, you know, and always before, he was the one that did the kidding. 'C'mon, Frank, you know I always wanted to be a doctor. . . .' "

It might have been the only time in his life his humor had failed him. But instinct rarely fails for long. Within weeks, still in the hospital, he was having those cigars smuggled in, lying in bed in his nightgown, telling jokes, blowing out smoke.

"I walked in this one time—I'll never forget this, it was just so like the guy. He had that cigar in his hand, you know, and he's waving it up over his head like he does. . . .

"Well, he takes one look at me, gives this big wide grin. And then he just says one thing. Real proud, like he's been saving it all day.

" 'Me, and Red Auerbach.'

"Can you beat that? I mean—I mean, really? The guy's lying there dying, smoking his cigar, pretending he's Red Auerbach."

11

There has been a murder on the Hill.

It is mid-autumn 1994. Murder, even on the Hill—which, as a neighborhood, may be the safest in St. Louis—is not so rare as it used to be. But this one is different. There has never, in the memory of anyone here, been anything to match it.

An eighty-seven-year-old man, Joe Monti, has just confessed to the shooting of a sixty-one-year-old midlevel mobster, Frank ("Chico") Parrino, nearly three months before. Parrino was shot to death at the wheel of his car, in broad daylight on a Sunday afternoon, outside the tavern he owned, at the corner of Macklind and Dempsey. His wife was sitting next to him; the killer wore no disguise.

Press coverage was heavy and nearly unanimous. Parrino had been an "underworld operative"; the killing was a "mob hit."

What was remarkable: everyone on the Hill over sixty knew different. It was partly because of this, after several days of bungling, that the media finally got it right.

Joe Monti, it seems, used to own a bar of his own, the Savoy

Gardens on Wilson Avenue, in the 1950s. And in that bar, one night in the fall or early winter of 1956, Monti and Parrino got into a fight (nobody can recall over what). Parrino, twenty-three then to Monti's forty-nine, tore the older man apart, sending him to the hospital with a broken jaw and a face that needed stitches. Monti swore he'd get even. He'd been swearing it ever since.

All this the Hill knew, long before the police or reporters. And when Parrino got shot thirty-eight years later, twice in the head at point-blank range, there wasn't much doubt as to who was behind it or why.

Frank Borghi and Gino Pariani, sitting together in the waiting room of the Calcaterra Funeral Home, take turns filling in details. The story, even that day—it has been three months since the killing—is in the papers.

"Joe, he'd been walking around with that grudge thirty-eight years. There wasn't anybody around didn't know it. And he woke up that morning—maybe his jaw was aching that day—and he just said to himself, 'I'm an old man, gonna die soon anyway. It's time I got my evens.'

"So he just took a walk on up the street—he only lived a block away—turned a right on Elizabeth, and walked around the alley. He mighta been on his way to church, or maybe comin' back, or something. . . .

"And he walked up to Chico where he was sitting in his car, and he asked him—'Chico,' he said, 'are you open?' 'No, Joe, we're closed already,' Chico said.

"So Joe—he usually carried a gun with him anyway; he was kind of a feisty old guy—he just put that gun to him, shot him in the head two times. Right there, right there in front of Rae Ann.

"They don't know what they're gonna do with him. They got him at home right now, with one of those bracelet things around his ankle. It's not like he's gonna hurt nobody; he's just a harmless old man. . . .

"He got his evens, though, didn't he? He always said he would, and he did. It took him thirty-eight years, but he squared the score."

．　．　．

Things are like that on the Hill. Even today. Neighbors know neighbors, and neighbors' sons and cousins, and who's in St. Ambrose on Sundays and who's not. Armando Pasetti, in his seventies today, still sells prosciutto out of his uncle's ninety-year-old store. Sister Felicetta Cola, at the Sacred Heart Villa, today teaches the grandkids of the first students she had. On Saint Joseph's Day every March, the old women of the parish still teach the young ones the recipes of their youth; the breads and sauces are prepared together—again—and the recipes live on.

Tresette and briscola are still played in the taverns; the St. Louis Bocce Club, with its five hundred members, is full most nights of the week. And on one block of Bischoff Avenue, the proudest on the Hill, only five of twenty-four houses have changed hands in forty-four years.

In the end, though, it will probably be a losing fight. The Hill is old, and getting older. More than half its residents today are seniors. Of the thousand families who belong to St. Ambrose, fewer than one in four has a child in school. Much of the housing is ancient: turn-of-the-century "shotgun" houses, brickfronts with underground kitchens that no one but the inured would live in today.

"I'd give my house to my kids, but they don't have it in their hearts to live on the Hill," said Roland DeGregorio, a former Hill mailman—who for seventy-odd years has lived nowhere else—to a local news reporter two years ago. "My wife and I were born and raised here, and we will die here. . . ."

And when they do, they will be buried by Frank Borghi—and recalled, in jokes and stories and small backward glimpses, by their neighbors and relatives, for a generation after that.

Just like Joe Monti's old grudge against Chico: on the Hill, almost nothing is forgotten. The past, for good or bad—for today at least—is a living force.

In the early 1970s, the building of Interstate 44 resulted in the razing of several blocks of Hill homes—most of them along the mail route of Roland DeGregorio.

"The highway took ninety-eight families," DeGregorio said later. "A few died. They were so heartbroken, they died. They came to this country and that was their first house. . . . Taveggi's wife—she died. Taveggi's mother . . . his father who was born and raised here. They died."

It could have been much worse. The Interstate, as planned, was to have bisected the Hill—stranding 450 families on one side, away from the heart of the neighborhood, with the closest access a mile away.

Father Salvatore Polizzi of St. Ambrose, together with a handful of locals whose only real value was their fear, traveled to Jefferson City in September of 1971 to ask the state highway commission to build an overpass.

"The highway cuts the people off from their church" were the words of the first speaker and of the second. The commission's decision came the same day: there would be no overpass. The highway would go forward as planned.

The Hill turned to its best-known native—Joe Garagiola, born and raised on Elizabeth Avenue, former Cardinals' catcher, by then host of the *Today* show. Garagiola phoned John Volpe, future ambassador to Italy, at the time secretary of transportation in the Nixon White House:

"I explained to him . . . people like my mother could be trapped on the other side. The Hill must be helped. If those ladies are cut off from going to church, from the store, they will die."

The Hill got its overpass. When the news was announced from Washington, the bells of St. Ambrose pealed.

Every Wednesday, as they have for the past eight or nine years— none of them can recall exactly when it started—the Ravens meet at noon in the lobby of the Calcaterra Funeral Home.

The first order of business is to decide where to have lunch. Bartolino's, Pietro's, Guiseppe's, and Gianpepe's are the usual candidates, though there are sometimes one or two more. This is usually settled by a brief debate, other times by a coin toss. Except on weeks when one of them is celebrating a birthday; at these times, the birthday boy alone makes the choice, then is treated to lunch by the group.

The choice this Wednesday is Pietro's. Their table, set for ten—there are two visitors this week—has been readied, along a wall near the entrance, out of the flow of busboys and the business crowd. It is easily the best table in the house.

The waiter, a middle-aged man named Frank Pisano who has been working here as long as any of them can recall, greets everyone by his first name—but respectfully, without pretension, as you might greet a favorite uncle. He takes the lunch orders; five of the eight order catfish, which, when it comes, will be longer, and at least half as wide, as the plate on which it is served.

They are the same eight, more or less, every week. There used to be more of them, and the faces then were apt to vary from Wednesday to Wednesday. But as the years have thinned their numbers, those left behind find fewer reasons not to come—as though mortality might be tricked by keeping the lunch count steady. And these days, the seven or eight who show are most of those still left:

Frank Borghi, perhaps the hub of the group; Vince Di Raimondo, the Raven's old left fielder; Dom Italiano, crack bocce player, former minor-league catcher with the Cincinnati Reds; Frank ("Chickie") Severino, self-appointed Hill historian, lover and collector of anything in the image of Mickey Mouse; Ed Berra, former guard for the Ravens basketball team; the cousins Gene and Joe Mazzuca; and Dom Marfisi, Frank Borghi's old army buddy, Joe Mazzuca's former best man.

The youngest (Berra) is sixty-five, the oldest (Joe Mazzuca) seventy-one; most are clustered midway between. They are full-haired, thin-haired, and balding; fat, strapping, and pencil-thin; prosperous and struggling; dignified, joke-a-minute, and shy. At least one was a brickworker. Another is president of a bank. They are as different, or alike, as any eight men you would pick at random from a crowd.

And yet they have shared marriages, christenings, graduations, moving days, illnesses, jailings, and too many funerals to count. They have been best men, godfathers, and pallbearers to those now passed; they will be pallbearers to each other when the time comes. They have known one another, on average, sixty years.

("There was this story about us in the paper one time"—one of the lunch crowd will say later that day. "And it said how we were 'former Ravens' or 'Ravens as kids,' or something or other like that. . . . But the guy who wrote that, he got it kind of wrong. We were Ravens as kids—yeah, but so what? We were Ravens as grown-ups, too. We're still Ravens as old farts; we'll be Ravens the day we die.")

Their first clubhouse, in the mid-1930s, was the basement of the Borghi family home. From there, it moved across the street, to the "casket room" of the Calcaterra Funeral Home. Borghi, at the time, was club treasurer; the dues ("for candy and Cokes, or sometimes little parties") were five cents—then ten cents—a week.

They won their first trophy, for junior softball, when most of them were in seventh grade. It sits today, on a shelf by itself, in the den of Frank Borghi's home: "Ravens, St. Louis City Softball, 1939" is the inscription on the base. Above this is a ten-inch-high, brass-plated simulation of a golfer completing his swing. The golf club has been broken off at the base, to allow for the possibility that it might once have been a bat.

"They didn't have a lot of money for trophies back then," Borghi explains. "Probably somebody donated it or something, so they got it for free."

These days, their game is bocce. They play it, as devotedly as they meet for Wednesday lunches, at the St. Louis Bocce Club, every Tuesday night in teams of six—then talk about it, first for an hour through late-evening coffee at Armand's Pancake House, then through half of lunch the next day. ("We're still kids," says Dom Italiano. "I been tryin' to tell you that. It don't matter our ages, we're still kids. . . .")

This week, though, the Borghi-Italiano team have been 15–0 victors. So, while there is some fairly naked gloating ("What do you think, Chickie? Maybe a handicap next time?"), there's not a lot of room for debate. By the arrival of the catfish, the talk has turned to other things:

The Joe Monti murder case ("Nobody's gonna miss Chico, that's for goddamn sure"; "But hey, it's still murder, Dom, eighty-seven years old or not"), Michael Jordan, the St. Louis Sabers, the Washington University soccer team, the future of the NBA . . .

And other, closer things, too. Dead pals, old feats, triple bypasses, prostate problems. The sad fate of an old soccer ref named Pete ("always fair, always called a good game"), now far gone with Alzheimer's, whom one of them has just been to see:

"He's just sitting there on the floor in that place, up against the wall, eyes as blank as a stone, just rocking back and forth. So I tug on his trouser leg just a little. 'Soccer, Pete, soccer,' I say, 'let's play some soccer, whaddya say?' But nothing happens, there's nobody home. . . ."

Alzheimer's, they all agree, is the worst. Their least-favored way to go ("to feel your mind slipping like that," says one; "I tell you, I'd end it before I got that far gone"). There is some talk about Jack Kevorkian. Someone asks about Bobby Annis, Frank Borghi's old teammate, who is faring badly and will be gone in four months.

Mortality, it is plain to see, is on all of their minds. But no more so than their sons or their grandkids, or yesterday's bocce game, or the winter trips they have planned. And not nearly so much as the high, happy, long-gone times that link them—that are the only real reason for Tuesday's bocce or Wednesday's lunch.

"We had some times," Frank Borghi says, midway through recalling the well-remembered softball season of 1939. "We had some times. Rich, happy, you wouldn't believe. We're a bunch of lucky guys. Every man here, he's a lucky guy. . . .

"Dom there, we enlisted together, at the old Jefferson barracks—same day, spring of forty-three. . . . Vince, he was the shortest guy on the team. When I was managing, I used to have him bat leadoff; the strike zone was so little, he'd draw a walk half the time. . . ."

The lunch ends with a Joe Garagiola story. Garagiola, for fifty years, has been a hero to every boy and man on the Hill—every one of whom has his own favorite tale of "Joey G." Today's is one of the classics. But to hear it told, you'd swear not a man there has heard it before.

"There was this old Italian guy, right? This old guy from the neighborhood. And he says to Joe one day—it was right after Joe got famous, before he got on TV, when he was still playing ball for the Cards. . . .

" 'Hey, Joey,' the old guy says to him, 'You the first guy what comes from the Hill, with a name that end *a, e, i, o, u,* who getta name in the paper and no killa somebody.' "

They all laugh like thieves. Then the check is passed around. Seven of the eight throw cash on the table—it is Dom Marfisi's birthday week.

"Happy birthday, Dom," two or three of them say—softly, with surprising earnestness—and there are handshakes and hugs all around.

"But hey," somebody says then—and every man there knows what's coming next: "wasn't it just your birthday last month?"

They leave, as they came, laughing. Berra and Borghi to finish their workdays, the rest home to wives and grandkids, gardens, scrapbooks, travel plans, the telephone. The two visitors, on the street outside Pietro's, are invited to next Tuesday's bocce match.

"You come, we'll show you some things," Joe Mazzuca says. "Show you the game, maybe teach you how to play. You come, you'll see for yourself—we don't do bad for old guys."

12

Some time in the first three years of the 1880s, five Lombard immigrants—Luigi Caloia, Luigi Oldani, Luigi Berra, Luigi Genazzi, and Guiseppe Calcaterra—lost or quit their jobs in the lead mines of Union, Missouri. They made their way forty miles northeast to the levee of the Missouri River in north St. Louis, where they then inquired about work. They found jobs the next morning: at the Evens and Howard brick kilns on the banks of the River des Pères.

For a while, the five slept in a boxcar. After a week or a month, or six months (the record is there, but dim), a German family living on a hill in the area then called Cheltenham—inhabited at the time mostly by Germans and just-freed slaves—rented them a one-room shack. The family across the way was named Schloessel. The youngest Schloessel, Hugo, was five years old at the time. Ninety years later, as part of a collection of oral histories—*Immigrants on the Hill*, by Gary Mormino, published in 1986—Hugo Schloessel retrieved his memories of those times:

"There was a bunch of colored people living over there, and they were awful reckless, you know. And the first Eye-talians come over here . . . About half a dozen of them got together, and rented a house and batched it. . . . And the Germans who were here then—they mistreated those first Eye-talians. . . .

"In the evening they had an accordion. They played music sitting out in the yard and singing, and us kids used to hang on the fence listenin' to 'em. We thought it was funny because we didn't understand it. Then after a while, they sent for their friends and their brothers. . . ."

By 1890, there were ten shacks of Italians, 175 men in all, on the hill in Cheltenham. They had christened it, by then, La Montagna—climbing it, up and back several times a day to refire the kilns, it had seemed to them more like mountain than hill.

But by May of 1901, when the *St. Louis Post-Dispatch* ran its first of many tributes ("Successful Cooperative Colony in St. Louis"), it was officially—and for fifty years after—Dago Hill:

"Six hundred Italians, a community store and saloon, the North of Italy tongue, a $500 flag, a rented mass in a German-Catholic church, a Garibaldi society and an anti-Garibaldi society, Italian bread for the bakeries, and a $2 fine for fighting in a conspicuous place. All these things has Dago Hill unique among the communities of St. Louis."

They came, most of them, from the villages of Lombardy just west of Milan—Cuggiono, Castano Primo, Boscate, Ossona, Marcallo, half a dozen more—where they worked in the vineyards and silk mills, and had lived for generations on land they could never hope to own. Ten-year-olds, routinely, worked thirteen-hour shifts for a day's supply of rice.

"In the summer we started at four or five in the morning," one immigrant woman remembered more than half a century later. "There were no belts and no machines [in the mills] to turn the reel. The machines were us little girls. . . . In Cuggiono, we was so hungry we even steal from the pig."

The young men left first. They made their way to St. Louis, found work in the brick kilns, saved fifty or eighty dollars, then wrote home to their mothers in search of a bride. The mothers made inquiries in the village ("My son, he is doing well in America, is looking for a wife. . . ."), then mailed back pictures. The hopeful young men made their choices.

"So he wrote to me, 'Would you like to come and marry me?' " Maria Imo Griffero, a "picture bride" of fifty-six years before, recalled in 1973. "He sent me a picture, too. But when I meet him, more better than picture . . . was really nice and fat and dressed like a soldier. . . . So he sent money, so I went to a place in Cuggiono and got passporto. . . ."

The journey over was Dantean: the train from Milan to Le Havre, ten days at sea—in steerage, aboard *La Touraine*—between Le Havre and New York ("Never since the world began," a St. Louis reporter wrote in 1902, "have such loads of human freight been carried as those now being unloaded in New York harbor. . . ."); the daylong indignity of Ellis Island ("Who paid your passage? . . . Where are you going? . . . Are you an anarchist?"); and the final leg, again by train, to St. Louis from New York.

The trip cost, on average, sixty dollars—two months' wages in the kilns. But the reunions must have been something to see.

"Safe at last in the insular ghetto, families could celebrate," writes Gary Mormino. "Gifts were carefully unwrapped . . . a family Bible, a votive candle, a treasured heirloom. Maria Ranciglio proudly presented her husband with three sprigs from the ancient fig tree that had stood in their backyard. (In the Old World, the fig tree symbolized life, and after each child's birth the placenta was buried near the tree.) The nurtured sprigs grew into a tree at the rear of 5223 Bischoff Avenue, the Ranciglios' home for seventy-five years. . . ."

By 1908, there were 3,000 Italians on the Hill. By 1920, 4,000—more than a third by now native-born. The women kept house and raised babies; the men and boys, with steel picks and carbide lights, mined for clay underground.

"When I was fifteen [in 1916], I went into the mines to make shoes for the miners' animals," remembered Antonio Ranciglio, who had learned blacksmithing from his father as a boy. "Hydraulic Brick Company, they had five hundred mules to haul brick. Missouri mules—all white. The mules never came out of the mines. They went blind and died in the mines. . . .

"I make eleven cents an hour, ten hours a day. . . . Bad air, damp mines. The men who worked there all have bad lungs. When miners get old, they all walk like this . . ."

Almost no one stayed in school past eighth grade. More than a third were illiterate. As late as 1940, out of 1,600 men twenty-five and over living by then on the Hill, only seventeen would have a high school diploma. ("When hair begins to grow between the legs," goes an old Lombard adage, "one is fit then to marry and work.")

They were the lowest-paid, worst-educated immigrants in the city. They were also the most cohesive, the most frugal, the least divorced, the hardest working.

"You don't understand these immigrants like I do," Julius Selvaggi, by then in his eighties, said to Gary Mormino twenty-three years ago. "For a buck and a half they [worked] all day, ate garlic and onion and a half-loaf of dago bread, so that they could save the money and send it to the family. You don't know what these fellows went through."

Landless tenants through generations in their homeland, now—as the pinnacle achievement of their lives—they built homes: the cheapest in the city, out of wood shingles and cast-off kiln bricks. Most were on dirt streets; nearly half lacked flush toilets, a few had no bathrooms at all. They were worth, on average at the start of the Depression, $3,100 each. (The typical St. Louis home was valued at twice that amount.) But six out of every ten Hill Italians owned their own. No other immigrant group in the city—all of them better schooled, better paid—could say the same.

When Joe Garagiola signed with the St. Louis Cardinals, as an eighteen-year-old high school dropout in the spring of 1941, he was paid the bonus he had asked—five hundred dollars, the exact amount still owing on the Garagiola family home. As he recalls: "My brother Mickey and I, we took the check to my father, who was working at the kilns at Laclede-Christy. When he saw it, tears came to the poor man's eyes."

In 1902, they built their first church: St. Ambrose, on the corner of Cooper and Wilson Avenues—modest, wood-framed, with a fifty-foot steeple, all that $10,000 could buy. It became, overnight, the anchor for everything they believed in, took part in, prayed for, stood for, or sought to attain.

"We have many Catholic churches [in the city], it is true," the parish priest, Father Cesare Spighardi, told a reporter at the time. "But they are attended by well-dressed people, and the poor Italians who have no fine feathers with which to bedeck themselves do not care to mingle with them."

In 1921 it burned down. For five years after, they built it back: with children's dimes and parents' dollars (pledged weekly, over sixty months), the life savings of the parish priest, thousands of hours of free labor, tens of thousands of dollars in donated lighting, roofing, masonry, church bells, and tile. It was built of brick this time, and terra-cotta, with belfries and bays and ribbed vaults—eight times the size of the original, at twenty-seven times the cost.

On the day of its reopening, June 26, 1926: "Every flower was cut, and every home scrubbed, for the arrival of Archbishop Palica of Rome."

St. Ambrose was, to the people of Dago Hill, everything—almost literally—a parent can hope to be to a child. Home base, friend, provider, voice of wisdom, moral example, source of solace and strength. It was ten blocks from the home of its most distant parishioner. It knew everyone's business, was the first source turned to in any family's need or pain.

When Joe Garagiola, in the early 1940s, was offered his first tryout with the Cardinals, he didn't own a catcher's mitt. "None of our guys had one," he would remember twenty years later. "The only one we knew of belonged to Louis Cassani. He wasn't one of the boys. But Father Palumbo [the St. Ambrose parish priest] said that our Johnny Columbo knew Gino Pariani, who knew Louis Cassani. The network began operation, and we got our mitt."

"Rosemary and I, we were both christened there," Frank Borghi says today. "We were married there. Our daughters were married there. When we die, that's where they'll say the Mass."

13

It was the last good decade for immigrants in America. The last time our shores would be so welcoming, our cities so vital, our opportunities so broad. Soon would come the Great Depression, then the war—then the postwar throes of immigrant quotas, "urban renewal," blue-collar shrinkage, suburban flight. Cities would turn mean and faceless. Neighborhoods would be replaced by housing projects; "neighborhood" would cease to mean anything at all.

In St. Louis alone: Little Italy, Little Poland, the German section, Spanish Town, the Jewish "Ghetto," the Irish Tipperary and Kerry Patch—one or two were sick already by the time the Depression arrived; all would be dead, as neighborhoods, before two more generations had passed.

"The damn trucking firm bought the church and turned it into a garage," a St. Louis pastor would say half a century later, speaking of the demise of a Little Italy church—two years before his own parish would disappear, six years before he would be murdered by a gang of teenagers in the rectory of a third.

"In the future, all the cities all over the country will be condominiums. Where are those people going to go to church? . . . If I would be taken away from here, my heart would sink—twenty-seven years! I baptized kids over there that finally married, and I baptized their kids. You know, it's a family to me."

In *Immigrants on the Hill*, Gary Mormino's lovingly gathered book, there are few quotes that do not come from the mouths or pens of immigrants. One exception is on the book's final page, a single line from historian Kenneth Clark. Behind its truth lies the root of the Little Italy priest's anguish. And of the reasons that the Hill has survived.

"Civilization means something more than energy and will and creative power. How can I define it? Well, very shortly. A sense of permanence."

Dago Hill, from its earliest days, was a monument to permanence. No other neighborhood in St. Louis—perhaps anywhere—could approach its strength, its homogeneity, the loyalties it exacted from those who made it their home. Almost no one, once they had arrived there, ever left. No one worshiped or married, or was christened or buried, anywhere else but St. Ambrose. No one rented if they could possibly buy.

"Italians have gone to the Hill with the intention to remain," wrote the editor of a Little Italy newspaper—*La Stampa Italiana*—in 1927, at about the time his own neighborhood was beginning its decline. "They may move from a frame house to a more pretentious brick home; they may go from one street to another, but they stay on La Montagna!"

"Compared to the rest of St. Louis," concluded a study of midwestern immigrants published in 1911, "Dago Hill represents the best of America, and a vengeance for the name, 'Italian immigrant.'"

The Depression was a deathblow to scores of immigrant neighborhoods across America. For the Hill, it was a family experience.

"Grocery stores extended credit to the amounts of $200, $300. . . . Furniture stores waived payments, for months and sometimes for years," wrote Elmer Shorb Wood, in a 1936 Washington University master's thesis. "Friends made loans, sometimes to the point of self-sacrifice, and those who were employed spoke so often to their employers about a job for some friend, that their own were sometimes jeopardized."

Carolina Borghi—Frank Borghi's mother—for nearly sixty years swept the floors and answered the phones at the Calcaterra Funeral Home. She died in 1986, at the age of eighty-five. Ten years before that, she had been asked by Gary Mormino for her memories of the Depression.

"Honey, this is the Hill. . . . Like one family, the husband would run out of work, and another family would pitch in and bring food—only if it was a pot of spaghetti. . . ."

There can be peril in so much togetherness. By the mid-1920s, Dago Hill—in every sense—was an enclave. It had its own church, its barbershops, its fruit stores, bakers, grocers, and bars. (By 1915, of ninety-five Italian-owned "saloons" in St. Louis, more than forty were on the Hill.) With the opening of the Calcaterra Funeral Home in 1921, it no longer looked elsewhere even to bury its dead.

It was fifty-two blocks of north Italy. Poor, insular, uneducated, unmodern, proud to a fault. It took nothing from the city around it—except 2,000 pittance-paying jobs that the city was happy to give—and gave next to nothing back. Its boys and girls married only each other ("Marry women and buy oxen from your village only," the Lombard adage went). Its housewives went nowhere else to shop.

"Downtown, as far as [our] mothers and fathers were concerned, was the place you went to take your citizenship test," Joe Garagiola would write later. "Otherwise, it was as far away as the Duomo in Milan."

In 1919, Prohibition closed the bars. For most of the next fourteen years, in basements and garages the length of every block, a hundred homemade stills took their place. ("We had equal opportunity moonshine," Garagiola quipped once. "Everybody made it.") In the schools—already plagued, as one teacher had reported, by a "lack of legitimate amusements, a continual indulgence in alcohol"—teen-agers dropped out now not for jobs in the kilns, but to do sentry duty in their parents' basements or to run bootleg whiskey across town. Youth gangs turned suddenly violent. The Hill carved itself tighter; the streets grew less safe.

"Kingshighway . . . the creek . . . the railroad tracks—that was our boundary," remembered one Hill resident, Lou Berra, of his teenage years.

"Up the Hill we had the Blue Ridge Gang—Irish. To the north-west we had the Cheltenham Gang—a mixture of Germans and more-or-less natives. East of Kingshighway was the Tower Grove Gang, what most of us refer to as Hoosiers, people up from small towns. . . . Then the Dog Town Gang to the west. . . .

"You go beyond that and you get your ass kicked around. So you stayed within your limits."

It was 1925. Nothing much had changed in twenty years. The neighborhood was still 98 percent Italian, 90 percent unskilled. Still poor, insular, hardworking, still hoping for the best. But settled now, as neighborhoods go. And growing older. The first immigrants were just starting to die out. The flood had peaked fifteen years earlier; there were grandkids by now on the Hill.

And for the young—uneducated, unsupervised, with only a hand-me-down history ("When I was your age, in Cuggiono . . ."), no prospects to speak of, and no real sense of the land in which they lived—the future wasn't cause for much hope.

Sometime in the summer of that year, 1925—midway through Pro-hibition, in the final twelve months of the St. Ambrose rebuilding—a man named Joe Causino arrived at the church rectory to meet with the parish priest. Frank Borghi, at the time, was four months old; Gino Pariani was two years from being born. But both men, seventy years later (as would Charley Columbo and Peewee Wallace, if they could), call Joe Causino a saint. None of them, but for him, would probably ever have played soccer. But that's the least of it.

"What the guy did, really," says Borghi, "is, he saved a lot of kids. There's some people that say—and I won't disagree with 'em—that Uncle Joe, he saved the Hill."

Joe Causino was recreation director for the St. Louis Southside YMCA. What he saw in Dago Hill—as Gary Mormino, maybe a bit clinically, describes it in his book—was "an enclave in need of formal direction." What he must have seen, really, was a neighborhood of rugged promise—but with too many young second-generation Italians with no sense of tomorrow and too little to do with their todays.

His aim was to build a sports program that would include every boy on the Hill. And through that—as he was reported, nearly thirty years later, to have told a doubtful parent at the time: "to make these boys better citizens, good Americans. . . ."

"That's what we want," the parent is said to have replied. "We want our boys to be good Americans."

Joe Causino, to hear those who knew him tell it, was put on earth to help kids. "I'm 'Uncle Joe,'" he would say to each of them. "Never 'Mr. Causino,' always just 'Uncle Joe.' You remember that—we'll get along fine."

He tapped into their rivalries. He began with a street gang and ended with a softball team. By the close of the Depression, there were more than thirty "athletic clubs" on the Hill. ("The way it worked, it went by the street you lived on," says Gino Pariani. "I lived on Daggett Avenue—that was the Hawks.")

He found "sponsors" for boys in trouble ("you know," says Frank Borghi, "what you might call a big brother today, somebody to keep you straight, to keep you going forward"). He loaned money, found jobs, kept uncounted boys in school by making class attendance a condition for a spot on the neighborhood team.

"He was for clean living, for [making] good people," one of his first boys, Les Garanzini, remembered fifty years later. "He got us sponsors for each club—ours was the Fawns. . . . Then he had this clubhouse—he'd let us use the clubhouse for the whole weekend, thirty, forty boys. . . ."

He turned dry cleaners into team sponsors, St. Ambrose Church into the biggest sponsor of all. He converted YMCA buildings into clubhouses, found city money for playgrounds and soccer fields, then filled them as fast as they came.

By 1934, a thousand residents a day were using the Shaw School playground. Ten years earlier, the year before Joe Causino arrived, the number had been fifty-nine.

But he did more than build teams and fill playgrounds. He took a neighborhood's worth of boys whose idea of an ethnic divide was a "mixed marriage" between Lombard and Sicilian, and put them on soccer fields across from Irish, Spanish, Jews, Germans, and Poles. He helped join the Hill with St. Louis. He widened the worlds of 2,000 immigrant boys.

In the fall of 1928, the first all-Hill soccer team—under the banner of the Calcaterra Funeral Home—won the title from the Irish in the city's Foundry League. Ten years later, playing now in the colors of St. Ambrose parish, the Hill would win first place in the state.

"By 1941," Gary Mormino writes, "the Hill had become, partly through the medium of sport, an ethnic phalanx. Young and old, Lombard and Sicilian, old-world mustachioed Petes and new-world Yogis, passionately identified with the Hill, with St. Ambrose, with neighborhood teams."

"We had a closeness then," says Frank Borghi. "You don't see that kind of closeness anymore. Frank, Gino, Charley, Bobby Annis, the guys from the Ravens, all the guys from the Hill; I could name you a hundred names, five hundred names . . .

"You played for the neighborhood; you played for the Hill. And because it was fun. You won your games, you lost your games; you had your parties, maybe some tough times now and then. But it was always, always, just fun.

"The way it is today, you see these guys out there, they got twenty, thirty soccer balls, they're all serious, they're doin' their fancy drills, their organized calisthenics before every game. Hard to believe they're havin' much fun. . . .

"Us, we were lucky if we had one good ball. And calisthenics—I'd go get in the goalmouth, pick up a few rocks, shake 'em around a little to loosen up, and it'd be, 'Okay, I'm ready, let's go.' "

"The kids nowadays," Gino Pariani puts in at this point—the two of them are trading memories, along with Harry Keough, in the lobby of the Calcaterra Funeral Home—"the kids today, they stay home a lot more. Watch TV, hang out, maybe play a little ball or something with their dads. . . .

"There wasn't no TV then. And my old man, he didn't know nothing about games—he just worked (at the Laclede-Christy brick kilns, with Joe Garagiola's dad). Ten, twelve hours a day, six, sometimes seven days a week. He was hardly ever at home. And if he was—well then, he'd probably be sleeping. Or maybe he'd go down to the tavern, get himself a beer. . . .

"Us kids, we were never at home, except just to eat and sleep. If you weren't in school, you were always out somewhere—in the street, at the playground—always playing some kinda game. At least till you got old enough to go to work after school. And even then—

"The first year I went to work for Lungstras Laundry, there was this softball league in the afternoons, right after school got out, and I wanted real bad to play. So I asked my mother.

" 'Where's that ten dollars a week gonna come from?'—that was all she said. Oh, well . . ."

"Aw, don't be kidding the man"—Frank Borghi cuts in now, laughing softly and shaking his head. "C'mon now, Gino, you never let work get in the way of playing any game. . . .

"You remember those years you had that paper route [from 1952 to 1960, three to eight every morning, eight hundred papers a day], and you'd get to Sportsmen's Park, we'd be all out there on the field—and how you'd be still in your work clothes, and they'd be blowing the whistle to start the game?

"Remember that, Gino? Work never stopped you. You always made it in. So don't be kidding the man. . . ."

Both men laugh loudly. "Well, yeah," says Pariani, mock sheepish now, grinning at his old friend and rubbing his hands through what's still left of his hair. "I guess it did get to where I was a pretty fast dresser in those days."

To share time with these men—Borghi, Pariani, the Pietro's lunch crowd (Harry Keough too, for that matter, who played against them, sometimes with them, all his life, and grew up thirty blocks away)— to share their stories, their old rivalries, their hundred-times-told but still-laughed-at jokes; to hear them interrupt each other, contradict each other, laugh, flatter, cajole, pull one another's legs. It is the closest thing there is to looking at the past.

But not backward as history. A living past. Shaped by memories and shared rituals that are renewed—reshaped, then reshared—and grow dearer with every retold joke. A sense of permanence.

14

Joe Causino had been dead already thirty years on the night of April 25, 1981, when more than eight hundred of "Uncle Joe's Boys"—Ravens, Hawks, Stags, Fawns, Panthers, Gloom Chasers, Nightingales, Wildcats, and Wolves, a few as young as forty, the oldest maybe seventy-five—filled the Teamsters' Council House at 300 South Grand.

Borghi was there, and Pariani, and Charley Columbo, who was still alive at the time (though Peewee Wallace, former Hawk, had been dead two years by then). And the Hill's sports figures and politicians, and Father Polizzi of St. Ambrose Church.

One table was set for every team, two for some. There were toasts from every table, a dozen would-be toasters for every man who stood up. All the old local faces were there, some going back fifty years—as well as a few that no one in the room could recall ever seeing. Joe Garagiola, emcee for the evening, had come a thousand miles.

"We replayed a lot of games that night," Frank Borghi says. "All the big games, all the big goals—Macklind Field, Sportsmen's Park, the old WPA, the night-league softball games Charley and I used to play. We sure remembered some things."

They had come to honor Uncle Joe—"The Hill's guardian, god-father, and overseer," Garagiola called him in the toast he gave that night. But just as much, to honor themselves. It had been a hundred years since four Luigis and a Guiseppe had spent their first night in a one-room shack on Cheltenham Hill. Eighty years since they'd built their first church. Forty years since the day in 1941, six months before Pearl Harbor, when Richard Severino, standing next to a poster proclaiming that "Hitler Can't Get Our Goat," had led three hundred Hill youths in a pledge:

> I am an American. My father and mother was born
> in Italy, and because they did not have the chance to
> get to be the thing they wanted to be, they decided
> to come to a nation they had read about as a land
> where people could be anything they wanted to be,
> and go to any kind of church they wanted to, and
> stay home if they wanted to. . . .

And it had been ten years since the day, in 1971, when the sculpture by Rudolph Torrino—*The Italian Immigrants,* a man, woman, and infant child in baggy clothes with a single strapped-closed suitcase between them, Ellis Island name tags affixed to their breasts—had been unveiled in front of St. Ambrose Church.

The statue remains today. The life seed and symbol for a community, fewer and fewer of whose members—with every passing Sunday Mass—if they glance up at it at all in going by, have more than a history-lesson notion of who those three frail people were, of what message their silent, pigeon-splattered presence could offer today.

15

There was some talk, after that night we all had for Uncle Joe, of maybe doing it again sometime. Everybody there thought the same—that the way we all got together, with everybody having such a good time and all, that maybe we should make it a regular thing."

Frank Borghi is speaking, this time by phone, in the early winter of 1995. Just a week ago, he says, the Ravens celebrated Frank ("Chickie") Severino's seventieth birthday.

"Seventy, that's a big one. A very big one. And Chickie, with his wife gone and all, he's had some pretty tough times. We went to Gitto's, told a lot of old stories, had a good, good time."

And the same week as Chickie's birthday, he buried a woman 104 years old.

"Mrs. Gianinno. She lived on the Hill her whole life. She died at home. A lot of the old ones, like Mrs. Gianinno, they want to die at home."

A second reunion doesn't seem likely now, he says.

"I guess it probably won't happen. There's no plans anyway. It's been a while now. A lot of those fellows who were there that night, they've passed on, some of 'em maybe moved away. Charley's gone, of course. And I buried Bobby Annis last spring. . . ."

It is five days before Christmas. There will be thirty, he says, for Christmas this year: all seven children—three girls, four boys, the youngest thirty-two, the oldest forty-one—their two wives and two husbands, ten grandchildren, a sister of Rosemary's, an assortment of in-laws.

"But each of 'em, you know, they bring something with 'em—chicken, ravioli, a salad, whatever. So Rosemary, she won't have too much to do."

The Borghi home is made for big Christmases. It is two homes really, made into one. Eight or nine years ago, after raising seven children in three bedrooms and sleeping for years themselves on the living-room couch ("we had 'em stacked up in bunks, with a fan in the hall in the summer to cool down the house—but one of the kids, anytime the weather got hot, would always be stealing the fan"), Frank and Rosemary bought the house next door, connected it to their own with a family room, and went overnight from three bedrooms to six.

"Rosemary and me, we like different things. She stays up later at night, for one thing, and sometimes I watch sports on TV. So now—this way—we got space to ourselves. And when the kids come visit, like now, there's room to put 'em up."

From outside, the house seems massive. The inside is like a succession of irregularly shaped railroad cars.

"After the two was first connected, the cars going by on the street outside—every day, at least one or two of 'em, they'd slow down, back up, then stop and just kinda look. . . ."

The big event, every Christmas, is the "Secret Pal Cherry Pie." It goes back thirty-five years—to when the children were little and there was no money for gifts.

A month before Christmas, everybody would pull out of a pie the name of a "secret pal"—for whom each would buy his one and only gift. On Christmas mornings, the family would gather in a circle on the living-room floor, presents wrapped at their feet, and each one in turn would guess—from the size and shape of the packages, and what each knew about the others' wants—which present was for whom. The first right guess was the first gift given. It took sometimes half the day. It still does.

"When we were first starting out, there was nothing left over for Christmas or birthdays," Rosemary Borghi, who has taken the phone from her husband, is saying now. "So we made up games. 'Secret Pal' at Christmastime; and for birthdays, this game we called 'King or Queen for a Day.'

"We had this big cane chair, with velvet cushions. And the birthday person, he'd get to sit there on the cushion and have stuff brought to him and all. He'd be the 'king for a day.' And that's what we did instead of presents. We did that for years."

There were nine of them then. There are thirty today, and "Secret Pal" has expanded: two pies now—adults give to adults, children to children—and two circles. But it is still, for each Borghi, the heart of Christmas Day. When one of them can't be there (which happens rarely—of the seven children, only one lives out of state), he or she is included by phone, long-distance, for however long it takes.

"John [the eldest of the Borghis' children] called last year from Florida—I don't even want to think about the bill!" Rosemary Borghi is saying now. "Everybody had to speak to him, every single, solitary one. All of them giving hints, and him guessing—Is it this? Is it that?—and the yelling and the laughing, and the carrying on. You'd think they were still kids, the way they carry on. . . .

"But in all these years—thirty-five years!—I've never once heard anyone say, 'Oh, what's this for?' or, 'Why'd you get me that?' "

Rosemary Borghi had a quadruple bypass in October. The Ravens met for lunch that Wednesday in the St. Elizabeth Hospital dining room.

"To hear the doctors tell it, you'd think it was like getting a splinter removed; 'Don't worry, you'll be better than ever, better than ever,' you know how doctors like to say. Well, let me tell you something—at my age, you don't 'better-than-ever' so fast."

She's had other problems too, over the years—diabetes, a mastectomy—though if you met her and didn't know otherwise, you'd say she'd never seen trouble in her life. She seems, like her husband,

Frank, indomitable. Strong, pretty, gay-spirited, permanently happy. As though every day were Christmas and every minute a gift.

The two of them are talking about a trip to Italy in the spring: Palermo in north Sicily, where the Novaras—Rosemary's family— are from; Cuggiono, from where Frank's father, Carlo Borghi, like a thousand other young men before him, left for America sometime around 1910.

"I'm not exactly sure when he came over. But he fought in the first war [on the U.S. side], so it had to have been before then. He was in France during the war, I think. I was too—in the next war— and I always wondered if maybe we might have, you know, we might have walked on the same ground.

"But he died [of tuberculosis] when I was sixteen, before I ever went over, so I never got to know for sure."

It will be the first trip for them both. Neither one speaks the language or can name a single relative still there.

"But there's got to be some cousins or something," Rosemary Borghi says. "Somebody there who would know who we are. And anyway, it's where we come from. It's family. It's something we ought to do while we can."

But meanwhile, there is Christmas—five days away—with its houseful of Borghis little and big. And the chicken and ravioli dinners, the "Secret Pal" circle, midnight Mass at St. Ambrose.

And a week after that, New Year's Eve: at the Bocce Club this year—"with about thirty or forty close pals"—dancing to the music of the Jack Stevens Band.

"And after that I'm not sure," Frank Borghi says. "Except John"—who lives in Florida, where he works for Anheuser-Busch— "he'll be here on business for a while. So we'll see a lot of him, so that'll be good. . . .

"He's a maintenance supervisor, John is. That's what they call it anyway. It's a good job, I know that. He's real gifted mechanically; there's just about nothing he can't do. He's been home now three, four days, and already he's fixed the dryer, the icebox, the problem we had with the sink. . . .

"A lot depends on Rosemary, though. She's feeling pretty good now, but she gets tired kinda easy. So we gotta watch that. It's gonna take some time."

Then suddenly, out of nowhere, he veers: "Oh—and you know what else? It was just in the paper. They voted Harry [Keough] into the National Coaches Hall of Fame.

"And I'm thinking now—I'd maybe like to go with him to Oneonta [New York] when they give him that award. It'd be fun to take a trip with Harry again. It's been a long time. But that won't happen till June. . . ."

The phone call is half an hour old. It has been quiet—undisturbed—on the Borghi end till now.

Suddenly, there are two cries—simultaneous, both from small children. One sounds delighted, the other as though a nose has been punched.

"I think I gotta go now," says Frank Borghi. "Gotta go be a grand-dad, you know? But you have a merry Christmas, okay? [The cries are louder now.] Oh yeah—and a happy New Year, too."

And at that instant there are two more sounds—guitar chords, and what sounds like something breaking.

"Watch the tree!" an adult voice yells in the background. And the Borghi family Christmas clicks off.

16

Stanley Matthews, England's regular right-winger, was probably at the time the finest soccer player in the world.

Thirty-six years later, he is named by *The Ultimate Encyclopedia of Soccer* as one of ten "Legends" of the game: "a small elite group at the highest echelon of the sport, acknowledged by millions of fans as the truly great."

Matthews was, write the editors, "the first great soccer player of the modern era" and "without rival as the greatest outside-right in the world."

Thirty-five years old at the time, and midway through a professional career that would stretch past his fiftieth birthday, "the shuffling, mesmerizing genuis named Matthews" was the only player on the English side capable of single-handedly lifting any game—against any rival—to a higher plane of play. Against the Americans in Belo Horizonte that morning, had he lined up opposite U.S. left-wing Eddie Sousa, the Portuguese odd-jobber from Fall River, Massachusetts (and the weaker of the two Sousas on the U.S. side), it would have been a very different game.

But Matthews was in Rio—"resting" for the game against Spain. Beyond the fact that the English were certain of victory, it was never explained just why. (There had been rumors of a "slight limp" in the final stages of the game against Chile, though this never went further than the press.) And in the minds of their players at halftime—and of Walter Winterbottom, the English coach, whose decision it had been to leave Matthews behind—there had to have been at least the beginnings of doubt.

They were a historic team, even without him. Three others of that English eleven are included today among the *Encyclopedia*'s second-tier listing of the all-time "Great Players"—more than two hundred in all, from forty-four countries over nearly ninety years— who, in the view of the editors, fall just a shade short of the "Legend" standard but were among the best of their times.

Of the two hundred, twenty—including the 1950 three—are English; twenty-one are Italian; eighteen are from Brazil. No U.S.-born player, of any era, makes the list.

Tom Finney, twenty-eight years old, at outside-right (or outside-left, when Matthews was playing): "His versatility was matched by his skill. . . . 'Grizzly strong' . . . genuinely two-footed, as brave as they come. . . . A 12-year England career with 76 caps and a then-record 30 goals. . . ."

Stanley Mortensen, twenty-nine, at inside-left: "As fast over ten yards as any English forward, with finishing skill to round off the openings his pace created. . . . The first man ever to score a hat-trick in a Wembley Cup final."

Billy Wright, twenty-six, at wing-halfback: "By reading play superbly, timing tackles well, and leaping to remarkable heights for a smallish man—he extended his career for years and years. . . . The first in the world to reach a century of caps."

They had been culled from the best of the of the English club teams—Stoke, Blackpool, Arsenal, Liverpool, Manchester United— where they played for modest but more-than-meager sums (fifty dollars a week was about the average), practiced regularly, were coached superbly, and drew crowds in the thousands for every game they played. The least of them were national heroes. The best— Matthews, Mortensen—were on the level of saints.

Still, to have left their star player off the roster, for no clear reason, in a World Cup match—even against the United States—was a gesture of almost incredible arrogance. ("Hubris," one British reporter would call it later. "And the gods were watching from their posts. . . .")

One thing should be said for the Americans. For a team that was given—and gave itself—no chance of winning, they had left no stone unturned in their efforts to win.

For years by then, the English, and most of the rest of the world, had been playing in the so-called WM (or 3-2-2-3) formation: the center-halfback drawn rearward to play—as "stopper"—between the two fullbacks to buttress the defense; two of the five attackmen meanwhile also pulled back, into midfield positions, to line up between the halfbacks and the front three.

This created a four-tiered effect (not counting the goalkeeper): three front-line attackers, two midfielders directly behind, two halfbacks, three fullbacks in final defense of the goal.

The Americans, since the game had been invented, had relied instead on the mostly outdated 2-3-5 formation: two fullbacks, three halfbacks, five on the forward line—and were regularly thrashed to pieces by every European team they faced.

"When you play in that two-back system, you're leaving their wings open—and they're gonna kill you, they're gonna eat you alive," Frank Borghi says today. "With three backs, you're playing more man-to-man. One of their wings gets the ball, he's gonna have a man on him pretty much right away."

Simpkins Ford, in recent years, had experimented with the WM. Borghi, Columbo, Wallace, and Pariani all knew it, as did Philadelphia's Walter Bahr. And together, sometime before they had flown out of New York for Brazil, they had approached Bill Jeffrey—who wasn't a fan of the system but may not have cared much either way—and persuaded him to let them give it a try.

For seventy-three minutes, it had throttled the Spanish—until the U.S. players had been run so ragged it wouldn't have mattered what formation they were in. And today, through the first forty-five minutes, neither English winger, Mullen nor Finney—who may not have been prepared for a three-back U.S. defense—had had a lot of success.

. . .

So strategy may have played some part in the first half's outcome. Another element, certainly, was the void that Matthew's absence left. And then the God-sent freakishness of Joe Gaetjens's goal.

But beyond these things—which, by themselves, were worth perhaps a two-goal margin in a game that could easily be decided by ten—the difference was the U.S. defense.

They had played like a guerilla palace guard—except for Borghi, who had played, as one press account would say of him later, "as though he shared the goal mouth with his twin." Keough and Joe Maca had challenged every ball within range—dogging, charging, forcing the wingers, drawn wide, to pass from the corners and sides. Columbo, since the first minutes, had shut Roy Bentley down with shadowlike marking and who-knew-what mix of threats, gutter talk, and late hits.

(Bentley's play would later be described as "tentative." It's just as likely that he was simply scared.)

Only Stanley Mortensen had had some success. And that had been thwarted by Borghi, and by Mortensen's own, almost uncannily repeated miskicks.

When the teams took the field for the second half, the equation was different. Not dramatically, not even noticeably. It was nothing, unless you were looking for it, that you would have seen from the stands. U.S. play was still ragged and lurching; the English had lost none of their poise.

But there was a difference now. There was respect. And the presumption of respect—from both sides of the ball. The understanding, for the first time reciprocal, that this was a real game.

The United States lost control to open the half—carelessly, on a poorly judged pass by Joe Gaetjens with less than ten seconds played. The English took possession five yards behind the midfield line.

But they didn't slow play this time, or look to spread the field, as they had at the start of the game. There were no Billy Wright footwork exhibitions, no lateral dribbling runs along the midfield line.

They didn't shuffle or showboat or pass-drill, or wait for U.S. mistakes.

They played soccer. The United States played soccer. Each in its own way.

"They had to have figured that, by that time, they'd have been up three or four goals," says Harry Keough today. "They'd had some bad luck, some close shots. But that wasn't the whole story, and they knew it—it wasn't like we'd never been on their end of the field.

"By the time we got started for the second half, they had to know we were a little tougher than they'd thought."

For the first six or seven minutes, the rhythm seemed to swing between sides.

First the English. In tight, four-yard passing patterns—moving downfield as surely and tauntingly as raindrops drip between rivulets on their way toward the bottom of a windowpane. Until they reached the periphery of the U.S. zone. . . .

Then a steal, an interception, or (but only once in those minutes) another Borghi save, and it would be the Americans' turn:

Keough or Maca, or Borghi's rocket-launcher right arm—which could send the ball fifty yards in the air—up the sideline to midfield . . .

A two- or three-player knockdown, an English forward on his knees in the dirt—and Gaetjens or Peewee Wallace sprinting full tilt, on a mission for the English goal . . .

Never reaching it, never getting even close—stripped, or just blocked, by Alf Ramsey, to be tapped back to Bert Williams or sideways to Laurie Hughes.

And the English slow drip would start again. . . .

In U.S. football, dominance is sometimes measured by "time of possession"—how many minutes and seconds, out of a sixty-minute game, a team can control the ball. It is a useful but often deceptive statistic, only sometimes reflective of the outcome of a game.

There is no such measure in soccer. If there were, the 1950 English team would be a model of possession-time dominance: patient, time-eating, fluid, inexorable—in the mold, or close to it, of the early-1960s Cleveland Browns, who lapped the field in five-yard bites behind the wondrous legs of Jim Brown.

The Americans would be easier to type—the mid-1970s Oakland Raiders. Smash-mouth, erratic, opportunistic, quick striking, error-prone, their weapons were strength, surprise, intimidation, and the sneering, irrepressible grittiness of a quarterback they called "the Snake."

Eight and a half minutes into the second half, the United States was awarded a corner kick from the English left side. Peewee Wallace took it—a near-perfect drop into a knot of players five yards out from goal. Three or four of them leaped in unison; it was Joe Gaetjens's head that found the ball. . . .

And sent it, a hard-hit, straight-rising head-punch, three inches over the bar.

Bert Williams, beaten cleanly, slumped against the post in relief. Gaetjens slammed his fists into his thighs—savagely, both at once—then turned to walk away. From the stands, there was a second of silence, then cheers. Then something else.

"*Mais um*" a single voice shouted, from somewhere near the front. "*Mais um! Mais um!*" And then another, then four or five more.

It spread through the stadium as rapidly as a wind gust, or panic in a theater. From the front rows to the rear, from the English side upfield to the Americans'—ragged at first, then in unison—until every voice was shrieking it, a deafening, punched-out, staccato roar:

MAIS UM! MAIS UM! MAIS UM! MAIS UM!

They wanted one more. There were thirty-seven minutes still to play—and already they weren't looking just for survival, for the clock to run down quickly, for an eked-out American win. They were greedy now. They wanted a humbling. They wanted one more.

For every English ear that heard and understood them, it had to have been the lowest moment of the day.

17

"If I say the name 'Joe DiMaggio,' what's the first thing you say? 'New York Yankees,' right? You don't have to think twice. . . ."

Walter Bahr is sitting in his living room, just off the seventh hole of the Elks Country Club in Boalsburg, Pennsylvania, a three-hour drive northwest of the Philadelphia neighborhood where he was born, learned his baseball and soccer, and left when he was still a young man.

It is a large room in a comfortable house in open country, with a two-car garage in back. The room is hung with pictures, mostly of his athlete-sons.

He is talking about loyalty. It is something he talks about a lot.

" 'Stan Musial?' Simple. St. Louis Cardinals. 'Ty Cobb?' Detroit Tigers. You hear the name, you say the team—you don't have to think twice.

"But what if I say, 'Reggie Jackson?' You say Yankees? No good. He bailed out for the A's on a money deal. Pete Rose? Philadelphia—but he spent more time in Cincinnati. Franco Harris? Pittsburgh. But he wasn't there at the end. . . .

"It used to be, the loyalty was to teams. Ty Cobb was a Tiger, Babe Ruth was a Yankee; that was it. It was something you knew, you could count on. It was part of your world. . . .

"Today? I'll tell you—the number of Cal Ripkens left are few and far between."

This is the sort of talk you hear a lot of from old men. About how nothing lasts anymore, nothing is the same as it used to be. About how big money corrupts athletes and dilutes fans' loyalties, and takes the joy and the fun from the game.

Often, as they talk, such men turn slowly more bitter, their voices grow slowly more hard—until it is plain that it is themselves, and not the game at all, that they are talking about, that the only loss they are lamenting, really, is their youth.

"He has been a young man. He has been a hero. He has been adored and happy and full of animal spirits." John Cheever once wrote of such a man, a fictional, middle-aged former college track star named Cash Bentley, now reduced to reprising his low-hurdling glories, drunkenly, over the neighbors' living-room furniture, on suburban Saturday nights:

"And now he stands in a dark kitchen, deprived of his athletic prowess, his impetuousness, his good looks—of everything that means anything to him. . . . He feels like a ghost of the summer evening. He is sick with longing. . . ."

Walter Bahr is not such a man. He speaks without bitterness, and without longing, and only rarely (or when asked) about himself. His sadness—if it is sadness at all—is not for dead heroes or lost youth. When he speaks of loyalties, he speaks still from the heart of a boy.

"Stan Musial. Seven batting championships in—what was it?—fourteen years? Ted Williams, DiMaggio, Jimmie Foxx. And this catcher I used to like a lot: Frankie Hayes, from the old Philadelphia A's. I followed all those guys. . . .

"You take any one of them out of their uniforms, put 'em with some other team? I'll tell you—it'd have been like changing my name."

• • •

He signed his first pro contract at fifteen years old, with the Phila-delphia Nationals of the old American Soccer League, to play half-back for five dollars a game. Three years later, it was up to fifteen dollars; by 1948, it had reached twenty-five.

In the summers of the early 1950s, he played in the Canadian League for a team called the Montreal Hakoahs—thirty-five dollars a game, plus a sausage and a bottle of Canadian Club. If you count the food and whiskey, it was the biggest money he ever made.

Meanwhile, he taught history at a junior high school in Philadel-phia's Bridesburg—"the Polish neighborhood, mostly stevedores"— for $2,400 a year, coached college freshmen at $400 a season, and was a camp counselor in the summers between soccer games in Montreal.

Today, he is the father of two sons—Matt and Chris Bahr—who between them have earned probably ten million dollars kicking field goals in the National Football League.

Both began as soccer players—in the summers at their father's camp in the Adirondacks, in Saturday-morning leagues at the high school where he taught. ("I never coached 'em, really, not actually coached 'em; just gave 'em tips.") Both, like him, became stars. One was all-American; another—says his father—"should have been." A third son, Casey, played on the 1972 Olympic team.

But the times by then offered different options. Chris Bahr, a hard-kicking Penn State soccer halfback, signed with the Cincinnati Bengals, as a field-goal kicker, in 1976 for a starting salary of $40,000 a year—an eighth of his income by the time he was through.

"You're a kid, twenty-two, twenty-three, just coming out of col-lege, and you get offered that kind of money? The heart may say, 'play soccer,' but the pocket talks louder. And it says—'football.' "

He's not a bit critical of any of this. He'd have done the same him-self, he says. Still, to listen to him talking through the course of an afternoon, it's plain that he feels there's something missing in the world his grandkids will come to know.

"I was watching this TV program a while back. A baseball show. And they had these old-timers on—Musial, Ted Williams, Duke Snider. And the three of 'em, they're talking, you know, big-league baseball, about the plays and the great games and all. . . .

"But the thing of it was, the more you listened—they could have been talking about soccer, or sandlot baseball, or any other game they'd played as kids. Because what was different—they talked about the *fun* they had. Not the money, not the fame, not even so much about how the game was played . . .

"What they talked about, what they remembered—I mean, here were three of the biggest names in baseball, and I swear, you could have been listening to three little kids—what they remembered was the *fun*."

Walter Bahr is rounder today than he was as a youth. Not large exactly, just with a roundness about him. Round face, rounded shoulders, an oval head that finishes in a long forehead above which is what remains of his hair, which is silvery gray.

You would scarcely know him from the smallish, sharp-featured, intent-looking young man who stands shoulder to shoulder with Harry Keough in the back row of the 1950 team shot.

He was a husband already by then, and a father. His first son, Casey, had been born the year before. And a teacher, and a coach, and a camp counselor. And a twenty-five-dollar-a-game soccer pro. He was carrying his first mortgage. He was twenty-three years old.

He is almost seventy now. Healthy, comfortable, accomplished, married fifty years. Nine years ago, he retired as Penn State's soccer coach. Four years later he watched his youngest son kick the winning field goal in Super Bowl XXV.

He smiles often, talks easily, and plays golf "every day that ends in *y*." His wife is vital, smart, and young looking. She covers the living-room floor in four-foot bounds. They talk to each other like kids.

His father was a door-to-door salesman for the Crescent Tea Company. The two were never close. He died when his son was eighteen.

"He was a father. He worked, he brought home the money. It was the Depression. That's what fathers did in those days."

His neighborhood, in the Kensington section of Philadelphia, then sometimes called Fishtown ("maybe because it had fish markets, it used to smell like fish, I'm not really sure why"), was English, Irish, and Scot. Its people earned their livings in the textile mills.

On the block where he lived—other than his father's—there were only two cars: "Mr. Cantwell, a policeman—he had one. And Mr. Roberts. I don't know what he did but he had a car. He usually had a flat, but he had a car."

Fishtown, to hear Bahr tell it, was a lot like Dago Hill. The mills were there, and the stores and taverns and schools. No one had much reason to go anywhere else. Almost no one ever did.

"You walked to school. When school was over, you ran to the playground—you had to run, to get there early to get in the game. There was always a game—soccer, half-ball, stickball, it could be anything, always something with a ball. . . .

"When the game was over, you walked home, you had supper. Then probably you went to the Boys' Club to play Ping-Pong or basketball, or maybe shoot some pool. Then after that you went home.

"Life was simple. For everything you did, you had three sets of clothes. You had your school clothes, your Sunday clothes, and your play clothes. That's all you ever called 'em, and you never confused the three."

The Lighthouse Boys' Club was founded in 1895, in two rooms in Episcopal Hospital, to serve the mill workers of Kensington—"to provide social rooms and a restaurant as a substitute for the numerous local saloons."

It may, for a while, have served in that role. If so, there's no one still alive who recalls.

"It was as simple as its name," says Walter Bahr. "It was a boys' club. It was a place for boys to go."

They went there, over the years, by the tens of thousands, beginning at eight years old. The dues (in Bahr's day) were one dollar a year. It was staffed, at no pay, by its oldest members. Parents were seldom involved.

"I was there every night. Everybody was. There was nothing you couldn't do—basketball, Ping-Pong, checkers, chess, a library, game rooms, a pool. I played sax in the club orchestra. I dove for their swimming team. I even boxed for a while. . . .

"On Monday nights they had dances. You paid a nickel toward the records, and for the coal to heat the place. A lot of marriages I could name got their starts those Monday nights."

There were rules: No smoking. No drinking. No cursing. No fighting. Hats came off at the door. "And you didn't break 'em, either; you didn't mess around. You did, and it'd be, 'Okay, let's have your card, fella, you're out for a week.' You learned to respect the rules."

The director for twenty-two years (and all of Walter Bahr's) was a man named Fred Woerner. There wasn't a boy at the club he didn't terrify—some long after they were boys.

"I've seen sixty-year-old men, thirty, forty years later, they'd be at some function or something, and Fred would come in the door. . . . Well, the beers go under the table so fast you wouldn't believe, and the cigarettes are gettin' stubbed out right and left. 'Oh hi, Fred, howyadoin'? Good to see you!' . . .

"Oh, but the guy was incredible. Incredible. During the war, you know what he did? He wrote personal letters to every club guy overseas. For the whole war he did that—regular, personal letters to two, three hundred guys. . . .

And every year a birthday card—it didn't matter how old you got. Hundreds of guys, I don't know, maybe thousands of guys. What he did, he put the dates in the stamp spaces on all the envelopes so he wouldn't forget, but you'd never see; then he'd mail out a bunch every day. Here I was, in my late fifties, still getting birthday cards from Fred. . . ."

(Fred Woerner resigned as director about 1950. As Bahr recalls it: "Times had changed by then; the club was strapped for funds. . . . It had to apply to Red Feather [a division of the United Fund] for help. But to get help, you had to conform to their rules. One of them was, the head guy had to be a college grad. Fred wasn't. So that was it—he lost his job.")

More than 13,000 boys came through the Lighthouse Boys' Club in Fred Woerner's twenty-two years. Most of them, at some point, on some level, played soccer. Soccer was a serious sport in Kensington in those days.

Four hundred boys every season, thirty-two teams at four age-levels on three fields. The top coaches and refs were recruited; English and Irish fathers—some of them themselves players with Hosiery Local or Fleischer Yarn—took afternoons off from the mills to watch their sons.

By February 1944, when the now long-defunct *Pic'* magazine devoted three pages to its coverage of the club (including a photo of the then-seventeen-year-old Walter Bahr having an ankle taped by the team trainer), it had already placed eighteen players on Olympic or World Cup teams.

"It is the largest single soccer organization in the world," the *Pic'* reporter wrote. "Only the armed forces of warring nations, using soccer as a training tool, field more squads than Lighthouse does."

"We were pretty good," Walter Bahr says today. "We had some great coaches, some really great coaching. Bart McGhee, from the 1930 World Cup team, a Scottish guy, he played for Bethlehem Steel in the thirties—he was one of my first coaches. Hal Blakely, he was another one. I think he played on the twenty-eight Olympic team. . . .

"A lot of those guys, they'd be Lighthouse guys as kids, to begin with; then they'd go on to play in the Olympics or the World Cup or something, or maybe as pros; then they'd come back and coach at the club. That's how it was. The club had been good to you, you got to be a certain age, it was time to give back. . . .

"Guys, people—there was loyalty then. To the club, to the neighborhood. . . . The older kids would coach the younger ones; the younger ones would get older, they'd remember, they'd give back. That's just how it worked.

"We had some great athletes come out of the neighborhood in those days. And not just soccer, either . . .

"Bobby Thomson—he hit the big home run in the World Series—he was one of our guys. Walt Masterson, he pitched for the Washington Senators. Jimmie Wilson, I think he played for the Cubs. Dick Spalding, Eddie Stanky—you remember Eddie Stanky? He wasn't from Kensington, though. He was was from Nicetown, the Polish neighborhood, the next neighborhood over from ours. He was with the Dodgers, I think, or the Giants. . . ."

(Lighthouse celebrated its hundredth anniversary, at the Canstattar Club in Philadelphia, in June of 1995. "We had four hundred guys there, maybe more," Bahr reports. "The average age was probably seventy. The oldest was ninety-four—Harry Rogers, he's been a referee seventy years, keeps a record of every game he's ever reffed, and every score. He's retiring next year, though. Says he's getting too old. . . .")

The longer he talks, the more you notice—how little he says of himself. Or of his teams, or their wins or scores or records, or any of the other things old athletes brag about. He was a great soccer player. He is in the Hall of Fame. He was a pro at fifteen, and for twenty-three years after that. His sons have been national heroes, his daughter was a college-champion gymnast; he coached four undefeated teams at Penn State.

But instead he talks about the neighborhood and the neighborhood's boys. And the Boys' Club and the coach he had when he was twelve.

False modesty is common among athletes—the strikeout pitcher who credits his infield, the four-touchdown quarterback who "couldn't have done it" without his three-hundred-pound blocking buddies on the offensive line. This sort of talk is cheap and painless. It's expected from heroes; some of the time at least, it's sincere.

But with Bahr, it isn't that. It's simpler than that. He is a man who, for so long and from such an early time, has been part of something larger—and for whom that sense of linkage is so defining, so built into his being—that it wouldn't occur to him to think in any other terms. About himself or anyone else.

"John and Eddie Sousa, they didn't think of themselves as Portuguese. They thought of themselves as Americans, from Fall River. I wasn't German; I was from Philadelphia—Kensington. Frank and Harry, they were from the Hill.

"If there was ever any sense of loyalty, it would be to where you came from. 'How could they pick that guy from St. Louis? We got a better guy from Philly,' that sort of thing. . . .

"Oh, there was an Irish club, and a Scottish Club—the Philadelphia Bluebells. That was the Scottish one. You could say they were ethnic clubs, but that was never any big thing. They were just players who happened to be Scottish or Irish or Jewish or whatever. . . .

"You might be talking about somebody and you might say, 'that Irish bastard' or 'that Jew bastard,' but it had nothing to do with him being a Jew or an Irishman. He was just a bastard, who happened to be a Jew or a German or whatever.

"It was a neighborhood thing. Nobody thought of it any other way. The only other breakdown, besides between neighborhoods, was between the publics and the Catholics—and that just depended on where you went to school. . . .

"I was from Kensington. That was it."

Walter Bahr and his wife left for the suburbs years ago—in the early 1950s, not long after their first child was born. ("It seemed like the right thing at the time. The housing was cheaper outside of the city, and it's good for kids to have grass.") But as soon as young Casey got to soccer-playing age, his father started taking him back.

"On Saturdays we'd drive into town, to the old neighborhood. I'd take him to the Boys' Club so he could play with 'em, be a part of the program, get a sense of what that was about. His brother, too, for a couple of years.

"I guess I thought they'd missed out on something, not growing up there. They wouldn't say so, if you asked 'em, but I would. So maybe that was it. Maybe I was trying to make up for what they missed. I'm not sure just what, really. It's more a feeling than anything else, a sense of things being a certain way. . . .

"When I was a kid—if I broke Mrs. Lambert's window? Mrs. Lambert, she wouldn't have to worry; she knew my dad would come and repair that window for her. There was no question. Everybody in the neighborhood knew that it was my ball that had broke Mrs. Lambert's window. . . .

"You learned that stuff early, what you could get away with—and you couldn't get away with much. Everybody knew everybody and trusted everybody. And had fun together. That's what a neighborhood was.

"So I guess that's part of why I took the boys back there. Trust, closeness, loyalty, being a part of something. You don't see a lot of that stuff anymore."

"You know, I hear myself saying all this—about how it was better in my day, and all that. And I start thinking that maybe it's just an old guy talking, that maybe I'm just showing my age.

"But you know, I just thought of something Casey said to me once. It's been maybe ten years ago now. . . .

"He said he remembered when he was still a little kid, and I was traveling a lot then, playing a lot of soccer, and he used to tag along with the team. And how he noticed that we were always laughing and joking, and hanging around together after the games.

"And that it always seemed like so much fun. He said he figured it'd be like that when he got old enough to play.

"But it wasn't. 'Our teams were always too *serious*' is what he told me. 'Our teams never did that. We never just had fun.'

"But, hey. At least he saw it, right? He saw the value. So maybe there's still hope for it, huh? Maybe there's hope for having fun."

18

Three minutes had passed since Joe Gaetjens's missed header. U.S. play had flattened. For all but thirty seconds since then, the English had owned the ball.

But by sound alone, you'd never have known it. The crowd would not be stilled:

MAIS UM! MAIS UM! MAIS UM! MAIS UM! MAIS UM!

They roared. They roared so loud they pitched. You could see it from the field—30,000 seated bodies pitching, recoiling, then pitching again with every exhaled roar. A forest of spasming, perfectly jerking shoulders and heads. The old stands swayed with the noise and motion. Flags waved, shirts waved. The air itself seemed to move.

MAIS UM! MAIS UM! MAIS UM!

The English were magnificent. They seemed neither to hear nor see. Pummeled from three sides by derision, friendless in a foreign stadium alive with its thirst for their fall—and now thirty-odd minutes from defeat—they seemed not even to know.

The only real clue was on the sidelines. Walter Winterbottom

115

plugged his ears with tissue. His bench players, heads lowered, cupped theirs with their hands.

But the on-field eleven were as steely as chess masters. They simply played soccer. It was something to see.

More and more now with every possession, they took the game to the wings; short, upfield passes a yard or two inside the touchlines that kept the U.S. defenses pulled wide.

The wing play opened the middle. Mistakes were more costly, the field—like a fought-over jungle—became an ally to those who used it best.

Three times in six minutes, a U.S. defender charged too soon or too close—and footed the ball out of bounds. Each time, the English throw-in came deeper inside the U.S. zone. The field receded surgically, in six-yard bites.

But the English, that day, weren't finishers. It was much as before: the deeper they took it, the less room was left on the wings.

Until finally, each time, with the field running out, came the inevitable centering pass—and the goal-front jam of crashing bodies, as rhythmless as a brawl. And all three times, within not too many seconds, the U.S. side's clearing kick.

The Americans were infighters. The English were not. It had been the difference so far.

But the Americans were tiring now. It was starting to show. Their own possessions were less wide-open, less unfailingly downfield. They side-passed more often. Their forwards looked for halfback outlets; the halfbacks passed among themselves. Charley Columbo's face was as red as the stripe on his jersey. Joe Gaetjens, between runs, held his sides.

It had happened, just this way, against Spain. For seventy-eight minutes they had played transcendently. Their defense had bullied the Spaniards; their attacks—like today's—had been few, but sudden and reckless, and had seemed to those watching to have come from thin air. Off one of them, in the twenty-third minute, had come the Pariani wing shot that—for fifty-five minutes after that—had been the only score.

Through all of it, they'd kept surging—kept hitting, kept punishing themselves. There'd been no hint of a letdown, no sign that the balance would swing. And when the score remained 1–0 with the game more than eight-tenths gone—as Harry Keough, years later, would say—"we were the only ones in the place not surprised."

Then, with twelve minutes to go, the Spanish had tied it. And the Americans, instead of mustering, just collapsed. Two more goals followed quickly, and what had almost been the upset of the World Cup became instead, as one reporter would write, "a creditable effort from a talented fledgling team."

On the field four days later, with the same 1–0 lead and twenty-eight minutes still to play, there couldn't have been one among them who wasn't having thoughts of Spain.

"We didn't have the conditioning those guys had," Harry Keough would say later. "We were good for maybe twenty, twenty-five minutes before we started to tire. And when you start tiring, when the lungs start to go, it's tough to stay focused. It's tough to keep the will alive."

With seventeen minutes gone in the half, the will was still alive.

But then, in the eighteenth, when Stanley Mortensen ran by Joe Gaetjens in the center circle, and Gaetjens turned to give chase—and looked like nothing so much as a lame old hound in pursuit of a hare—the *MAIS UM!*s faded to nothing so fast you'd have sworn, to hear it happen, that the English had scored.

They didn't score. Eddie McIlenny intercepted a Mortensen cross that was meant for Roy Bentley ten yards out from Borghi's goal. And the United States, one more time, cleared the ball.

But what had happened was powerful—the first sure sign of limits being exceeded, of something breaking down.

You see it sometimes in the final rounds of a prizefight, when a fighter's legs go suddenly wobbly or his arms begin to drop; or in the fourth quarter of a football game, when—for the first time all day—a hard-used defensive line collapses backward, a hole opens, a runner goes through untouched.

Such moments, in themselves, are rarely game breaking. The tired legs survive till the bell; a linebacker closes the hole, makes the tackle, prevents the first down. But they are the first sign. The beginning of something inexorable, like cancer or an avalanche. And you know, when you see them, that they will end in defeat.

The crowd noise edged from roars to buzzing. The Americans seemed deflated. The English played on, unfazed.

Clarkie Sousa, alone among the U.S. forwards, still seemed fresh.

There was no explaining why. He was no fitter than any of the others; he'd run as far and as fast as any man on the field. But to hear his teammates tell it, it was almost always this way.

"Clarkie, he never got tired," Harry Keough says. "He could run all day; he just never seemed to wear down."

It may have just been because of the player he was. He was the best—there's not one of them today who doesn't say so. The best dribbler, the surest passer, the purest talent on the team. He did things with the ball that no one else could—and the same things with less effort. So it stands to reason that he'd be fresher by the end.

"It was like Peewee Wallace always used to say," Keough remembers. "Clarkie, he was the only one of us who could take the ball and just go around anybody, just run away from 'em, just leave 'em standing there. . . .

"I've seen him do things you wouldn't believe if you saw. . . . He'd just kinda drift the ball up, bounce it a couple of times on his knees, then bounce it up top, and run around guys with the damn ball on his head. On his *head*, I swear, on his *head*. . . .

"Amazing. The guy was amazing—unique. I never before in my life seen a guy who could dribble like that, never before or since."

It was two minutes or so after the Gaetjens embarrassment, with twenty-six minutes left to play, when Clarkie Sousa began his effort to be the lungs of the team.

It came first off a clearing throw by Frank Borghi, to Joe Gaetjens at midfield. But the ball never reached Gaetjens. Sousa ran ten yards cross-field to get under it, then stole the ball, literally, on his chest in the air.

From that point on, he played the midfield like a ranging wolf. He took clearing kicks and halfback passes off the toes of his teammates; he shadowed tiring forwards, became an outlet for any man with the ball. When Pariani went down, in the twenty-third minute, following a collision with Tom Finney at center field, Sousa swept up the caromed ball so gracefully it could have been a parlor trick.

Ten seconds later, and thirty yards farther upfield, he passed across to Peewee Wallace—whose shot over the English crossbar ended the only U.S. attack in fifteen minutes of play.

Four more minutes passed. Three more English wing attacks, each one fully crafted, fully executed, sixty yards from point to point. Each one, more than the one before it, made a mockery of the U.S. defense—then a mockery of itself when it tried to move off-wing.

The first attack ended in a missed header, by Finney, from the penalty mark twelve yards out from goal; the second on a save by Borghi—when he came ten yards out of the goalmouth to intercept a cross. The third when Harry Keough stripped Jimmy Mullen, as neatly as a pickpocket lifting a wallet in a mob.

Between times, as an English paper later would report it, "The Americans fiddled with the ball."

It was more ambitious than fiddling, but the end result was the same. And with one good pair of lungs among five forwards, it would have been hard to do more.

They were taking an awful beating. And with an eternity still to play. Eighteen minutes. Far too long.

There were no cheers at all now. Only sporadic, collective exhales—*AEEEAHHH!*—whenever yet another English shot went wide or high, or was saved or blocked or kicked clear.

And in the last several minutes, some applause. Applause now, not cheers—civil, scattered, subdued, nothing at all like the roars of before.

They applauded Clarkie Sousa's scoop-up of Pariani's ball at midfield. And Borghi's heroics, and Wallace's too-high kick. They applauded sometimes, as well as exhaled, when a new attack was repulsed.

It was appreciation now, more than rooting. The way you might

119

applaud the courage of a beaten-dizzy fighter, who refuses to fall but has no chance at all to win. Part of you, even as you cheer him, wants the fighter to go down—to stop the carnage, to get the moment done. To put an end to that stupid, stubborn bit of hope that won't go away but that you know, in the end, will be squashed.

They applauded now, every chance they had. It was just that sort of applause.

$$\boxed{19}$$

To get to the University Lakes mobile home park, you take the Florida Turnpike west out of Miami past the Dade County line, until it puts you onto Southwest Eighth Street. Then follow that ten minutes till you come to the University Lakes Shopping Center, which is just past 127th Avenue and impossible to miss.

The sign for the park is on your left. The trailers—or "buildings," as the lady in the front office is wont to call them—are everywhere you look.

There are 1,250 of them, spread neatly over more than sixty acres, separated by streets with numbered names. Clarkie and Anita Sousa live at number 1458 Southwest 127th Court. They have lived here twenty years.

It is a warm November day, sunny and windless. On the patio outside their trailer—the two are joined by a low-hung postered roof—are arranged several chairs and two small tables, on one of which is a pitcher of Coke.

"We keep beer for guests," Anita Sousa says. "And some stronger stuff too. But we never touch it ourselves. Just once we did. It was a real hot day; we thought, what harm would it do to split one beer? One beer. Well, you know what happened? You guessed it. We both passed out in that hammock over there."

On the side of the trailer away from the street, a narrow lawn slopes down to a wooden dock at the edge of a bright green cove. It looks perfect for swimming—"but you gotta be careful," Clarkie Sousa says, and chuckles, his eyes widening in a parody of fear. "There's alligators in there. We see 'em sometimes, right from here."

There are palm trees everywhere, and grass and water and blue sky. Their street has next to no traffic; however near or far the neighbors, there is no sense of them at all. It is not what you think of when you think of a trailer park.

Clarkie Sousa is seventy-six years old. He could pass for sixty—and only his face shows that. He is bald (he has been bald since his twenties), just short of six feet, broad-shouldered, angular, deeply tanned. His legs, under blue shorts, are long and thin and muscled—a runner's legs, you would say if you saw them, though it has been years since he has run. There is not an ounce of fat on him. His chest and stomach form a nearly perfect plane.

He moves as easily as he must have at forty, stands and walks at full height. He is, still, every inch the athlete. It is hard to imagine, contrasting the vision of the 1950 team photo with the Clarkie Sousa of today, where and how the body has aged.

"He was a star. He won't say it like that, not just in those words, but Clarkie—any team he played for, he was always the star."

Anita Sousa is a petite woman with milky white skin. She is the same age as her husband. She looks, if it's possible, the younger of the two. She is still pretty. Her hair, however she manages it, is still red. To see her, you'd swear she was Irish; she looks like Ireland itself. But her parents were both born on the same Portuguese island—Saint Michael's, in the Azores—that her husband's parents are from.

"It's a good thing I'm here. Because Clarkie sometimes, he won't talk for himself. But I don't mind telling it. I watched—I don't know, how many?—a hundred, two hundred of his games. . . .

"I used to hate it sometimes. It could be awful watching; it could be the worst thing you could want. Because the other team, no matter who they were, their first job was always the same: 'Knock out Clarkie Sousa. However you got to do it, get Clarkie Sousa outta the game.'

"I used to sit in the stands, and the people around me, they'd be yelling, *'Hit him! Hit him! Hit him! Get him out!'* And they'd be throwing oil cans, soda cans, whatever they had to throw. There'd be days sometimes, I'd sit in the stands and just scream and cry. . . .

"But not everybody. Clarkie had his fans. I remember after one game, this fellow came over. 'Are you John Sousa's wife?' he asked me. I said yes. I didn't know if he was going to hit me, or scream or insult me, or what he was going to do. 'Well then,' he said, 'I just want to shake your hand.' "

Sousa, through all of this, has been smiling softly, leaning forward in his chair, absently scratching at the little bit of hair still left around his ears.

"I guess I was pretty quick," he has said once. "They didn't get to me too much. Hardly ever." Then, for the next two or three minutes, he has let his wife go on.

But now, suddenly, he leans forward, puts both hands to his mouth, and folds back a lower lip that has a pencil-thin line, a scar more than fifty years old, through the middle of its inside.

"That's where I got this. A fella kicked me in the mouth—split it clean open down the middle. Nineteen forty-one, in Ponta Stadium, against the Mexican all-stars. They got me that time, they got me good. . . .

"I tried to quit . . . when I was thirty-eight. I told 'em I was through, that I'd had it, but they talked me back. . . .

"The problem was, it got harder and harder to stay out of the way. I got hit more; I began to notice I moved slower. And it got so finally I couldn't keep my temper anymore. So I quit. I quit for good. I was forty-four then, I think.

"Nowadays, a guy does that—throws those kinda clips I used to get all the time—they give 'em a yellow card. Yellow cards, red cards—what all they call 'em. Today, a guy throws a clip like that, they give him a card, they throw him out of the game.

"Not then. Then, you got hit, you kept playing. You settled that stuff on the field.

"But it got so I got tired of being hit. So I quit. Other than that, I coulda kept playing."

They met at sixteen, in the summer of 1936, at the Casino Ballroom in Fall River, Massachusetts—the waltz, foxtrot, and Lindy Hop for ten cents a night, a quarter on Saturdays.

He had quit school a month before, to work as a weaver's apprentice at a local textile mill.

"That's all there was in town, was mills. And the way it worked was, you had to get somebody to speak for you, to say they'd teach you the trade. And if you did, well then they'd take you in—and you'd go in as a learner, and your guy would teach you, and you'd learn the looms and how to run 'em and all. But you wouldn't get paid. No sir, you wouldn't get paid.

"Then, after a certain amount of time, if you learned okay and the plant was doin' good, then they'd give you a certain amount of looms, say eight or nine looms to start out. And that was when you'd start getting paid. . . .

"What happened with me was, just when I was about to get my looms, the mill closed down."

And so, at seventeen, he enrolled at a technical school to learn pattern designing. He finished the course, but there were no jobs in town for designers. So he took the only one he could find—for nine dollars a week, as a presser with Shelburne Shirts.

All this time he was courting Anita, who lived with her family on the north side of town. He lived with his on the east side. The trip between took forty-five minutes on two buses; the fare was a nickel each way.

"Sometimes I'd have it and sometimes I wouldn't. Usually I wouldn't. So I'd walk."

His wife has been in the kitchen, replenishing glasses. She returns now to the patio, just in time to set her husband straight.

"No Clarkie, you always took the buses. That was why you used to always be so broke."

"Sometimes I didn't," he says.

"You always said you did."

"Well, sometimes I didn't." He is grinning. There is no rancor in his tone.

"Sometimes I walked. Musta been close to five miles, took more'n an hour each way."

Anita Sousa is back in her chair now, staring out at the dock and the water, swizzling the ice cubes around in her glass.

"Oh, I used to worry so much. I used to be always worrying and figuring. . . .

"Like if we wanted to go to the movies, I'd figure out how many times we'd been to the Casino, and how much that'd cost, and how much was gone for Clarkie's bus fare, and all of that. . . .

"And then, if there'd be nothing left, I'd tell him I'd get us a free ticket, 'cause I knew the man that ran the movie house. Oh, I had it all figured out."

Clarkie Sousa and Anita Madeiros were married June 5, 1940. He was still working as a shirt presser; she'd taken a job in a sewing factory for twenty-seven dollars a week.

When she'd been there six months, she was offered a penny-an-hour raise. "I told them to keep it. So they raised it to two cents. So what was I going to do?"

Those were hard years for Fall River. For mill cities everywhere. There was a closing a month through the worst of the Depression; the mills that stayed opened offered only long hours and pittance pay. But there was nothing else. And for the Irish and Portuguese immigrants who made up most of the city in those years, any job was a benediction. The sewing and weaving of fabric was synonymous with life.

"Everyday at six in the morning would come the first sirens," Anita Sousa recalls. "All the mills all over the city, their sirens would go off at six. If you weren't there by six, you were late. Then again at noon—that would be for lunch. Then at one o'clock—the end-of-lunch siren. And the last one at five, when the mills closed down for the day.

"You got so after a while you didn't hear it anymore. But if a stranger would have come into the city, he'd have thought there was an air raid going on."

It was soccer, at least as much as textiles, that kept them afloat. It paid bills otherwise unpayable. It was a backup against plant closings; it bought them things that other young mill couples only read about in magazines:

"Our first refrigerator. Remember that, Clarkie? Our first Frigidaire? Look at him. He's laughing, he remembers; he's just pretending he don't. . . .

"A hundred forty-nine dollars. A fortune. But the team, God bless 'em, they paid him three dollars a week to play. He'd get paid every week on a Sunday—and every Monday morning, first thing, I'd be down there with that three dollars, puttin' it down on that new Frigidaire. Our first big purchase. It made me feel like the queen of England. I swear."

Always before then—nearly all his life—he had played the game without pay. First as a kid in the early 1930s, for Arruda's Grocers. Then for a club team (The Lincolns), which, to hear him describe it, was a cover of some sort for a local gambler named Tiago Silvia. And there were others in between.

Then came the Portuguese Sports Club of Providence—and the three-dollar-a-week Frigidaire. From then on, the money he made on the soccer field began to compete seriously with the money he made in the mills.

There may have been no other American player, in those early years of U.S. soccer, who made the game work for him the way Clarkie Sousa did. But there was no one else, either, who was more brilliant at the game.

"I was very quick. Agile, I guess you'd say. That was the gift I had. The ball, it used to seem sometimes like it was just part of my foot."

. . .

Sometime in the early 1940s, he got out of the shirt-pressing business and went to work for Firestone, making gas tanks for the war effort overseas. In 1944, he went to war himself—aboard a converted tuna fisher ("they called 'em 'Yipees' ") delivering supplies to Pacific troop outposts: Guadalcanal, the Green Islands, Okinawa.

He saw no action himself and was back home—and back at Firestone, this time making friction tape—by the summer of 1946.

He had a five-year-old daughter by then. The Firestone job was paying him thirty dollars a week; he was making another fifteen on weekends playing soccer. Life seemed settled, and as sure as could be hoped.

But four years later, they were gone. In New York now, their second daughter just born, living in an apartment in the Ridgewood section of Queens. The fifteen dollars a game had risen to fifty; his Firestone wages had increased by half. Both blessings were the doing of one man.

"Rick Miller. He was a millionaire. A big man, a very rich man, the sort of man that can have what he wants."

And here he stops, and shakes his head slowly, remembering—perhaps marveling—before going on.

"And what he had was a soccer team. The German Hungarians. He was the sponsor; that was his team. And he had a mill, too: M&S Knitting, in the Queens part of New York. . . .

"He gave me a job as designer—designing patterns for women's sweaters in his mill. And as foreman too, later on. Forty-five dollars a week I got paid for that. And another fifty for playing on his team.

"So there I was, making more money playing soccer than I was at my job. So how about that?

"But he was happy, I think. I don't think—I *know* he was happy. We won a lot of games. There's only ever been three teams, I think, that won the national amateurs and the national open championships, both, in one year. And those German Hungarians I played on was one.

"That man, he treated me like a son. He told somebody once—I can never forget this—he said to him, 'I'd loan John Sousa a million dollars and never worry about him paying me back.' That's what he said. 'Course he never did. . . .

"But it was almost as good. I was working two jobs, and one of 'em was more like play. And Anita was working [at the old May's Department Store in New York] and getting paid pretty good. And we were saving, and not spending too much—we were never big spenders. And the dollars, after a while, they started mounting up.

"That's how come we got here. We came down one year on vacation, and we liked it, and we'd saved enough, so we just decided to stay. I was fifty-six then, the year I retired. That's been twenty years now, pretty close. . . .

"We've been lucky. The Millers, they were generous with us. Between the knitting mill and the soccer and all the rest they did, we got ourselves here.

"Fifty-six. Not a lot of people when I was growing up walked away at fifty-six."

He seems a different man now. Three minutes earlier, through his wife's telling of a story of the road trips she used to take with the team ("some of 'em—the married ones even—they had girlfriends in every town"), he had sat, quietly smiling, his tanned face tilted out toward what still remained of the day. The most spirit he'd shown was half an hour before that, when he was talking about the alligators in his cove.

Yet now, suddenly—as sudden as anything ever is with him—he seems on a roll. He talks about old teammates, the designing of sweater patterns, the many kindnesses of the Millers, the making of Depression soccer balls ("You ask the butcher for a bladder, you blow it up, wrap a cloth around it tight"). At one point, for fully two minutes, he describes the routes of the walks he and Anita take every day.

He is a different sort of man than his teammates. More reflective, more serene. He offers no scrapbooks, no triumphal soccer memories. It doesn't seem, from hearing him talk, that he even follows the game anymore.

The only relic of his playing days (or the only one in sight) is on the back of a shelf in the trailer's little living room: a small silver trophy from the Soccer Hall of Fame.

"I gave the rest to my daughter. I had no real use for 'em, and she'd been asking for years." (Before the next year is out, he will give her this one too.)

Other than that—and his trimness, and the athlete's grace with which he still moves—there would be no way of knowing that this was once the finest American forward ever to dribble a ball.

There is a second difference. It perhaps explains the first. Unlike his teammates, he has left all that behind—twenty years ago, when his home became University Lakes. It is dead for him now. In some ways—the important ways—it is dead itself.

"We went back to Fall River, for three years in the seventies, right before we came here. I worked for Bristol Knitting—it was the last job I had.

"We were thinking then we'd probably stay. We had family there. We knew the town, we'd grown up there, and all that. . . .

"We didn't like it no more. It had changed. It seemed smaller—it seemed crowded and small. A lot of our friends were gone, and some of the family. And most of the mills by then, they'd moved down south.

"And the neighborhoods were gone, broken up. . . .

"It used to be, in my day, the neighborhoods were kind of built around the church. The Polish had their church, the Irish had their church, the Portuguese people had their church, and so on.

"Ours, in the east end, was Spirito Santo. Anita's was Saint Michael's, in the north. And everything just kind of built in around that. . . .

"It was different when we went back. The churches were still there, most of 'em, but it didn't seem like they mattered much anymore. It wasn't the same feeling as before—less friendly, more crowded. Less like neighborhoods oughtta be.

"And after a while, it got so there didn't seem much reason to stay."

There is a sadness when he speaks of this. But it is not oppressive anymore—though it must surely have been at first. It is now more like an old scar. Like the scar on the inside of his lip: still visible, its source wound still recalled, but healed over now, no longer painful to the touch.

"What's that old saying they have," Anita Sousa asks now, "about how 'you can never go back,' or something like that?"

" '*Home,*' " her husband corrects her. " 'You can never go home.' "

"That's right, that's it," she says. " 'You can never go home.' Well, I guess we proved that right."

20

With eight minutes to go, came the moment. Heroic or shameful—or both, if such a thing can be—it was the moment that turned the game.

The score was still 1–0. The ball was in the center circle; two forwards fought for control. It squirted loose or was kicked; found the foot of Stanley Mortensen, alone on the right-outer circle, who took it on the run, dribbled by Eddie Sousa, then broke free.

He was at a dead sprint within seconds, up the center of the field. The nearest U.S. back—Charley Columbo—was three paces behind. There was only Borghi to beat.

Columbo gave chase, futilely. He was a fast runner; Mortensen was the fastest man on the field.

There were forty yards to be covered before the shot would leave his foot—from point-blank range almost certainly, at a goalmouth eight yards wide, guarded by a man with an arm-span barely seven feet across.

"In a situation like that," says Borghi today, "there's not much you

131

can do but guess. You guess one side or the other, and you dive. Nine times out of ten, you get beat."

Mortensen may not have known he had a close pursuer. Or he may have slowed just slightly to center himself for the shot. For whatever reasons, the gap didn't widen. It may even have narrowed by a pace. But it didn't close. And at the perimeter of the penalty arc, twenty-three yards out from goal, there was a body length still between the two.

It was at that spot that Columbo dove—at full stride, arms straight out from his head. And brought Mortensen down, like a felled tree, by his ankles from behind. It was a letter-perfect football tackle—as flagrant a foul as you'd see in a dozen soccer games.

"I didn't like it," says Walter Bahr. "I didn't like it at the time, and I don't like it today. But yes, I'd say it saved a goal."

The referee whistled play dead, then ran over to Columbo and shouted some words in his face. No one on the U.S. side was near enough to hear what they were.

" 'Bono! Bono!'—that's what Charley swore he said," recalls Keough, nearly fifty years later, with a laugh.

"Now, you couldn't always believe everything Charley would tell you. But the ref was Italian, that much was for sure. And the Italian team were contenders. And he didn't kick Charley out of the game, like most of us figured he would. So maybe it was true."

If the foul had happened another half yard upfield, it would have been inside the penalty zone—and the free kick awarded would have been direct: the kicker one-on-one against Borghi, an 80 percent certain goal. But the tackle had happened outside the arc. The penalty was an indirect kick, to be taken from the spot of the foul.

It was Alf Ramsey who took it. It was a chip shot, back-spun and perfectly distanced, that cleared the gathered wall of U.S. players by half a foot, then trajectoried down just behind them—to where Jimmy Mullen by then was waiting, in barn-door range of the goal.

Frank Borghi was a yard in front of the goal line when Mullen headed the ball. It bounced once, three yards in front of Borghi and a yard or so to his right, then rolled past him, a half yard out of reach, on its way into the side of the net.

He dove, missed, then dove again, backward—his body on the goal line by now—reached the ball with a finger or two, and slapped it wide of the net. But the English by then were hugging each other; Jimmy Mullen was kissing the air.

The Italian ref signaled his ruling: no goal. The ball hadn't crossed the line.

"Frank, he just reached back with his hand and flipped it out," Keough would remember, forty-four years later, to a reporter from the *Boston Globe*. "The English were screaming that it was a goal, but I was standing nearby. . . . The ball wasn't over the line."

But then Keough again, a year later: "It may have been over the line. To be truthful, I was not completely lateral to be a perfect judge."

Only a minute earlier, the English had owned the field. Their attacks were incessant—each one longer, more punishing, than the last. They played with the patience and sureness of a team ahead by six goals. The Americans had seemed stupored. The eight minutes still left had seemed years.

Even Columbo's tackle—except for the instant it happened—hadn't changed the sense of things. Only Mortensen had seemed unhinged by it, and even that had been brief. A few of the rest shook their heads briefly, or glared at Columbo, or cursed. Then they lined up at their places for Alf Ramsey's kick like a firing squad taking its posts.

But the kick's failure broke them. Utterly—in the single instant of the referee's call. For the last seven minutes, they never threatened again.

"They panicked after that, I think," says Keough. "They got desperate. They just sort of fell apart."

With five minutes left in the game, Peewee Wallace broke free upfield, drew Bert Williams out of position, and kicked point-blank at a wide-open net. A skidding Alf Ramsey, at the last instant, saved a second U.S. score.

MAIS UM! MAIS UM!

The crowd was back. They would stay now till the end.

. . .

The final bit of heroics is Harry Keough's favorite to tell.

"There was maybe three minutes left to play. We were dragging; we had nothing left. . . .

"And here comes Clarkie [Sousa], and he takes the ball at the half-line, and he just starts dribbling—and Billy Wright, he's with him, every step.

"But Wright won't charge him—he's scared of Clarkie; he's scared he'll get by—so he just hangs on, just stays with him. And Clarkie, he's eating off seconds, and we're all just thankful as hell. . . .

"The crowd was going crazy: *MAIS UM! MAIS UM!* But Clarkie, I don't think he was even thinking about scoring a goal.

"He just kept going like that—laterally—all the way from the half-line to the touchline on the other side of the field. And when he ran out of room—well, then he just kicked it off Wright's foot. The ball went out of bounds, and we got a throw-in from the side.

"All that took maybe thirty, thirty-five seconds off the clock, with three minutes left, and the rest of us beat all to hell.

"Thirty seconds was forever. Forever. That was an amazing thing he did. It might have saved the game. Nobody ever talks about it, though. . . ."

At the instant of the final whistle, the ball was in the air. Walter Bahr—in the center circle, the closest man to it as it fell—caught it in his arms, then held on. He would keep it nearly ten years.

(Bahr gave the ball, eventually, in exchange for a wristwatch, to the U.S. Soccer Federation. It is today on display in Belo Horizonte, in the stadium's trophy room.)

The crowd came over the side rails, in waves, thousands strong. No one tried to stop them. Within not much more than a minute, you couldn't see the field.

They had come for the Americans. They pummeled them, cheered them, hugged them, kissed them, draped some of them in flags. A small mob at one point, maybe two dozen men, slung Frank Borghi to their shoulders and paraded him, like a trophy, through the crowd. A minute later another band hefted Joe Gaetjens and did the same.

There is a photo of that moment: the striker and the goalie—the first and last heroes of the day—aloft on the shoulders of a mob of worshipful strangers after an impossible victory in a foreign land at a foreigners' game.

Borghi is spread-eagled, laughing crazily, draped over the bodies of his bearers like a too-long piece of bedding. Gaetjens is smiling—stuporously, like a shock victim or a man half asleep—half sitting, half lying across the rubble of shoulders below.

Both men look stricken. Both men look like boys.

21

The game's first hero was also its first to die.

"Once upon a time, [he] scored the most historic goal that an American ever put into a twine soccer net," a *Detroit News* columnist, Joe Green, wrote only two years ago. "And the result was the most astonishing upset in the history of World Cup soccer. . . .

"Then one day he disappeared, they say, with some men who carried guns."

There is more to it than this, of course. But much of it is hearsay. And what isn't hearsay—a young man dead, a widow left, three little boys orphaned—seems cruel and needless, and very sad.

Joe Gaetjens was twenty-six, an accounting student and part-time New York City dishwasher, when he headed Walter Bahr's kick past Bert Williams into the bottom of the English net, to become a hero to 30,000 Brazilians who, a day afterward, would not recall his name.

The next year, he went to France, to play for a pro team, the Racing Club of Paris—there's no particular record of that time. At twenty-nine, he returned to Haiti, where much of his family still lived, to open a dry-cleaning business in Port-au-Prince.

At thirty-one he married a Haitian girl. Three sons followed quickly—"he wanted to have a soccer team," his widow has said.

At thirty-nine he was dead. Murdered apparently, though that remains part of the hearsay. No one was ever accused; no body has ever been found.

In 1954, four years after the victory in Brazil, the U.S. team—of which Harry Keough was again a member—traveled to Port-au-Prince to play the Haitian nationals in a World Cup qualifying match. Gaetjens met their plane at the airport.

"He told us we'd beat the Haitians," Keough remembers. " 'Their coach has 'em all secluded, all locked up so they can't even breathe; he's got 'em living like monks. You guys should win easy'—that's what he said. He was right, too. We did beat 'em; we beat 'em two straight [though the United States, despite those victories, wouldn't qualify for the World Cup that year, or for thirty-six years after that]. . . .

"Before we left the island, he had us all over to his house. He seemed happy. He was still easy, still that same, free-spirit kind of guy. He was still Joe."

Within a year of that, he married Lyliane Defay. Around their house, in the hills that surrounded the city, he planted scores of rosebushes and a small forest of tropical fruit trees—nothing pleased him more than to plant a new tree, he once told a family friend. In the back-yard was a badminton court, which, by his death, his oldest boy, Jerry, had just begun to use.

He organized a youth soccer league. For a time, he coached the Haitian nationals, and L'Etoile Haitienne, the team he'd played for as a boy. At no time, according to those who knew him, did he show more than a passing interest in politics.

But his family apparently did, or had. It was the time of François ("Papa Doc") Duvalier, the voodoo doctor and self-proclaimed "president for life"—and of his dreaded, murderous personal police force, the Ton Ton Macoutes.

Papa Doc had won the presidency in 1957, and again—in a sham election, backed by money and guns—in 1961. The Gaetjens family, at least the first time, had supported his opponent, an industrialist and close family friend named Louis Dejoie.

Among Dejoie's advisers had been Joe Gaetjens's brother Gerard, who—according to a third brother, Jean-Pierre—would later be murdered by Haitian death squads.

On the morning of July 8, 1963, a Monday, two members of the Ton Ton Macoutes, accompanied by a Port-au-Prince policeman, showed up at the family's dry cleaners. Joe Gaetjens hadn't come in yet; his mother-in-law was managing the store. The three men waited. Sometime after that, he arrived.

"As Joe drove up, my mother tried to warn him," Lyliane Gaetjens told a reporter in 1994. "But he couldn't understand what she was saying. He couldn't think that anyone would want to do him harm."

He never got out of his car. The last to see him was his mother-in-law. A Ton Ton Macoute approached him, as she watched from across the street, put a gun to his head, and ordered him to drive. Three days later, the car, a blue station wagon, was found parked in front of police headquarters in Port-au-Prince.

There were rumors: that he'd been taken hostage in place of his brother, that the government had been angered by his defiance of a national strike. More than twenty years later, a former Haitian senator would claim that he'd shared a cell with Gaetjens—in a military prison, Fort Dimanche—and had been told later that his cell mate had been shot.

But the Duvalier regime, to the end, denied knowledge. He remains officially among the country's *disparus*.

His wife and three sons—the oldest then six—went into hiding the day he disappeared, and remained hidden two years before leaving the country for good.

In the early 1970s, the New York Cosmos staged an exhibition game at Yankee Stadium to raise money for them. The team's star, the great Pelé, implored the Haitian government—by then headed by Duvalier's son, "Baby Doc"—to open its books on Gaetjens's fate. There was no response from the government. No further efforts have been made.

His oldest and youngest sons, as of two years ago, were living and working in the United States. His middle boy, Richard, whose ambition was to make a movie of his father's life, died of cancer in 1993. His widow, Lyliane, at last report lived and worked in Washington, D.C. She is now seventy-one years old.

"The other night I was watching a replay of them carrying Joe off the field after his goal," she told a reporter two years ago. "The cameras went close in on his face. It was like Joe was still alive, and I was crying."

22

Belo Horizonte, Brazil, June 29—A sensation was caused here to-day when the United States beat England by one goal to none in the Association football match in Pool B of the World Cup. Probably never before has an England team played so badly.
                                        —*The London Times,* June 30, 1950

T he English were gracious in defeat. Privately and publicly, they congratulated the Americans. ("We could have played till next week and not scored a goal," Tom Finney told Walter Bahr on the field after the game.) They put on their best face at a postgame party, posed for photos with U.S. players in the airport the next day.

Then they flew south for their final game—against the Spaniards—lost quietly, 1–0, then flew immediately home. No World Cup team in history ever fell farther short of expectations, or returned home more shattered, in more abject defeat.

"Soon it was confirmed on the radio," British soccer columnist Geoffrey Greene would write later, "and shame-faced, self-conscious laughter went in a slow ripple round every public house in Britian."

One Fleet Street paper likened it to the defeat at Dunkirk. Another, the day the team returned home, bordered its pages in black.

On three continents, the U.S. win was page-one news. "The Biggest Soccer Upset of All Time," "The Kings of Football Meet Their

American Masters," "Mighty England Gags on Bitter Cup"—half the time with the same wire-service photo: "Young American goal-keeper, Frank Borghi, being carried aloft around the field by aroused Brazilian fans. . . ."

In the United States, maybe one paper in fifty printed a word: the *St. Louis Post-Dispatch,* courtesy of Dent McSkimming, who'd paid his own way south. ("He's smiling somewhere, in his grave today," says Harry Keough, "as big as soccer is now. He loved the game, but he was twenty years too soon.") A handful of immigrant weeklies. Some back-page, wire-service filler in the big-city sports pages—hard to verify today—that probably no one read. And that was pretty much it.

(*The New York Times,* as one account goes, got the wire report an hour before deadline—1–0, the United States over England. They suspected a hoax but lacked the time to verify. So rather than be duped, they printed nothing at all. Almost surely, no one noticed or cared. The day the story would have run—June 30—the United States went to war.)

The game, over the years, has been occasionally revisited. Usually around World Cup time, as a "color piece," to add historical balance to coverage of Cup play. Many of these have been sad efforts: Frank Borghi recast as a former "basketball" minor leaguer, the U.S. team as a "get-up" of foreign-born pros.

In 1966, just prior to that year's World Cup in England, veteran soccer writer Desmond Hackett published a memoir—"Oh! The Fun and the Fury I Have Seen!"—in the London *Daily Express* World Cup Guide. It's hard to imagine where he could possibly have gone for his facts: "On the dizzy heights of Belo Horizonte, a lush goldmine community, England suffered their greatest humiliation. They were beaten by America, a team that seemed to have come straight from Ellis Island, because there was not an American-born player on the side. . . ."

The Americans had a high time that Thursday night. There was a basketball game in town: Brigham Young University against some Brazilian college team. No one today can remember who or what, or how it came out—only that it started with the streets lined with screaming U.S. fans, and ended with a party somewhere. There was a lot of toasting. No one got much sleep.

The next afternoon they flew out of Belo Horizonte. Two days later, July 2, they played their last game, against Chile in Recife. They fell behind early, 2–0, scored twice to tie the game, then gave up three quick goals ("the heat really killed us that day," recalls Walter Bahr) to lose finally, 5–2.

Their World Cup duties were over. One win, two losses—to finish, tied with England and Chile at two points apiece, at the bottom of Pool B.

(Two weeks later, July 16, Brazil would play Uruguay—the final, deciding Cup match—in Rio's Maracana Stadium, with 200,000 in the stands. On a goal in the seventy-ninth minute, the underdog Uruguayans would triumph, 2–1. Next to the U.S. win, by then half forgotten, it was the biggest upset of the games.)

The day following their loss to Chile, they were invited to a July Fourth banquet at a U.S. navy base.

"A bunch of sailors," Keough remembers, "they got to riding Frank—'So you're the goalie for this fuckin' team, huh? And they [Chile] scored five goals on you? You must be one lousy goalie. . . .'

"So I said to 'em, 'Hey, you guys want to put some money on a softball game?'

"Well, Frank, Charley, Peewee, Gino, and me, we all played. Peewee was pitching to begin with, then Gino, then Charley after that. We *killed* those sailors; they never even *smelled* the ball. I won a thousand cruseros—bought myself a new pair of soccer shoes."

On Monday afternoon, they took off up-coast for Belém: a thousand miles, with stops in Natal, Fortaleza, São Luis. They arrived Tuesday; it would be Thursday before the first of them would get out.

("Killing Time Waiting" is how Harry Keough has marked these days—July fourth and fifth, 1950—on his handwritten calendar of the trip.)

They flew out of Belém on midnight planes—in three separate groups, two days apart. They drew straws for the seats available;

Keough won a spot in the first group but gave it away to Columbo, who was older and married, and worried about his wife. Joe Maca and Eddie Sousa, both day-workers, were worried sick—their bosses had expected them home four days earlier. They figured, by now, they'd probably lost their jobs.

Their trips averaged twenty-nine hours. They arrived home—to Philadelphia, Fall River, St. Louis, and New York—in twos and threes, between Saturday morning and Monday afternoon. Peewee Wallace's wife met one group at the airport; Gino Pariani can't recall if his wife came or not.

Harry Keough's plane landed at 5:00 A.M. Sunday. He was met at the airport by his father—then left for Peoria, to play softball, on a 9:00 A.M. bus. He was at the post office the next morning a little after dawn.

23

The eleven were never together again—though the paths of some of them, as teammates or opponents, from time to time crossed. All eleven played soccer at least through the 1950s, some for club teams, others as pros.

Eddie McIlenny played in England, then Ireland, Joe Gaetjens for two years in France. Bahr, Keough, and one or two of the others were together several more times on U.S.-backed teams, though never again in a World Cup, and never with much success.

It would be forty-three years before the United States would beat England again—in Foxboro, Massachusetts, in the summer of 1993. In the two countries' next four meetings, the goal tally would be 29–4.

Joe Gaetjens died first. Then Eddie Sousa, Peewee Wallace, and Joe Maca—none of them yet sixty years old—two years apart in the late 1970s. Then Charley Columbo, in St. Louis, in 1986. And finally Eddie McIlenny—"the Scottish mystery man," as Walter Bahr calls him—whom Bahr and the others tracked down through ads in British papers not long before he died, in East Sussex, in the fall of 1989.

. . . .

The five still left met six months later, in the spring of 1990, on the eve of that year's World Cup (in which the United States, for the first time since Brazil, would take part—and go home, winless, after three games). The reunion was in St. Louis, arranged and paid for by the London *Daily Mail*.

It was to be the usual retrospective—"the soccer sensation of all time, the day the giants were slaughtered"—though for British readers this time.

They met, as everyone always does, at Frank Borghi's funeral home, then had lunch together—along with Douglas Thompson, the English reporter—at one of the Ravens' regular haunts. Gino Pariani and Walter Bahr hadn't seen each other since their planes flew out of Belém, to separate destinations, forty years before.

"It's really quite a moment, to be together like this," said Pariani over lunch.

After lunch, as arranged beforehand, they changed out of their street clothes into uniforms that Harry Keough had brought—cleats, socks, jerseys, shorts, with the Olympic Games logo in front—then drove to a nearby soccer field. There, as a photographer snapped pictures, the five old athletes (aged sixty-one to sixty-nine at the time) dribbled, headed, chested, kicked, and saved.

Each man, in these photos, is bald or white-headed. Bahr and Keough are a little thick through the middle; Pariani is wearing sunglasses; the bleachers behind them are empty and small. But the ball sits up smartly on Clarkie Sousa's right toe, fully three feet off the ground. Borghi's two-handed save ("undertaker who has buried two of his teammates") is sure and full striding. In Keough's photo ("retired postman who still works as a soccer coach"), the ball drops neatly toward a drawn-back right foot.

Any one of the five pictures, if you drew a finger across the head, could be of a college star.

At the end of the day there was a final group photo: the same poses, in the same order exactly—allowing for their missing teammates—as in the 1950 team shot.

Borghi, Keough, and Bahr are shoulder to shoulder in the back row, hands clasped behind them, just as they'd been on the field in Brazil. In front are Pariani and Sousa, both kneeling, with a body-wide opening between them—and inside that a soccer ball—where Joe Gaetjens would have been.

The two photos are set one atop the other. "The victorious team" reads the caption of the 1950 eleven; "The surviving heroes" is written alongside the five.

"I don't know if we're heroes because we survived, or because we won," says Keough, with a chuckle that turns slowly to a laugh.

"Nobody knew us in 1950. Now it's forty years later, the other guys are gone, and we're heroes once every four years. . . .

" 'Better late than never, fellas'—I bet that's what old Peewee would say."